DYING

END-OF-LIFE CARE: A SERIES

SERIES EDITOR: KEITH ANDERSON

We all confront end-of-life issues. As people live longer and suffer from more chronic illnesses, all of us face difficult decisions about death, dying, and terminal care. This series aspires to articulate the issues surrounding end-of-life care in the twenty-first century. It will be a resource for practitioners and scholars who seek information about advance directives, hospice, palliative care, bereavement, and other death-related topics. The interdisciplinary approach makes the series invaluable for social workers, physicians, nurses, attorneys, and pastoral counselors.

The press seeks manuscripts that reflect the interdisciplinary, biopsychosocial essence of end-of-life care. We welcome manuscripts that address specific topics on ethical dilemmas in end-of-life care, death, and dying among marginalized groups; palliative care; spirituality; and end-of-life care in special medical areas, such as oncology, AIDS, diabetes, and transplantation. While writers should integrate theory and practice, the series is open to diverse methodologies and perspectives. Manuscript submissions should be sent to series editor Keith Anderson at Keith.Anderson@mso.umt.edu.

Joan Berzoff and Phyllis R. Silverman, *Living with Dying: A Handbook for End-of-Life Healthcare Practitioners*

Virginia E. Richardson and Amanda S. Barusch, *Gerontological Practice for the Twenty-first Century: A Social Work Perspective*

Ruth Ray, *Endnotes: An Intimate Look at the End of Life*

Terry Wolfer and Vicki Runnion, eds., *Dying, Death, and Bereavement in Social Work Practice: Decision Cases for Advanced Practice*

Mercedes Bern-Klug, ed., *Transforming End-of-Life Care in the Nursing Home: The Social Work Role*

Dona J. Reese, *Hospice Social Work*

Allan Kellehear, *The Inner Life of the Dying Person*

DYING

A TRANSITION

MONIKA RENZ

TRANSLATED BY

MARK KYBURZ
WITH JOHN PECK

Columbia University Press *New York*

Columbia University Press
Publishers Since 1893
New York   Chichester, West Sussex
cup.columbia.edu

Originally published as *Hinübergehen: Was beim Sterben geschieht* ©
(2011) 2015 Kreuz Verlag
Translation copyright © 2015 Columbia University Press
All rights reserved

Library of Congress Cataloging-in-Publication Data
Renz, Monika, 1961– , auhor.
[Hinübergehen. English]
Dying : a transition / Monika Renz ; translated
by Mark Kyburz with John Peck.
p. ; cm. — (End-of-life care : a series)
Translation from German.
Translation of: Hinübergehen : was beim Sterben geschieht. 2014.
Includes bibliographical references and index.
ISBN 978-0-231-17088-8 (cloth : alk. paper)
ISBN 978-0-231-54023-0 (e-book)
I. Title. II. Series: End-of-life care.
[DNLM: 1. Attitude to Death. 2. Terminally Ill—psychology.
3. Adaptation, Psychological. 4. Palliative Care—psychology.
5. Terminal Care—psychology. BF 789.D4]
R726.8
616.02'9—dc23
2015008493

Columbia University Press books are printed on permanent
and durable acid-free paper.
This book is printed on paper with recycled content.

Printed in the United States of America

c 10 9 8 7 6 5 4 3 2 1

COVER IMAGE: © Borut Trdina/Getty Images
COVER DESIGN: Diane Luger

CONTENTS

ACKNOWLEDGMENTS

I AM DEEPLY GRATEFUL to everyone who has assisted me in bringing to publication the English edition of this book. My warm thanks to Dr. Keith Anderson, whose enthusiastic response to "Dying Is a Transition" (*American Journal of Hospice and Palliative Medicine* 30 [3]: 283–290) made this book possible in the first place. I owe many thanks to Columbia University Press, especially to my translators, Dr. Mark Kyburz and Dr. John Peck; to Dr. Rudolf Walter, the editor of the original German edition of this book (*Hinübergehen* [Freiburg: Kreuz Verlag, 2011, 2015]); and to Dr. Miriam Schütt Mao, my research assistant, who supported and encouraged me time and again. I am most grateful to the following medical staff for their outstanding cooperation in the service of the patients in our care: Dr. Thomas Cerny, Department of Oncology, St. Gallen Cantonal Hospital; the palliative care physicians Drs. Florian Strasser and Daniel Büche; my fellow psychotherapist Michael Peus; and the palliative care teams St. Gallen and Münsterlingen. I am indebted to the following individuals: Dr. Gisela Leyting, a practicing supervisor, psychiatrist, and psychoanalyst; Dr. Ursula Renz, Department of Philosophy, Klagenfurt University; Dr. Roman Siebenrock,

Department of Theology, Innsbruck University; and Dr. Pim van Lommel, The Netherlands. I also extend my sincere thanks to my former teachers and colleagues, who were always prepared to discuss delicate questions in the areas of psychology and psychotherapy, theology, and spirituality. I owe special thanks to the many patients and relatives who shared their experiences with me. I wish to thank my family, my parents, my brothers and sisters. I would like to mention especially my mother for her critical comments and her unfailing support. My most personal heartfelt thanks go to my husband, Jürg!

DYING

DYING

INTRODUCTION

In Search of Inner Experiences of Dying

WHAT IS GOOD DYING? Is it perhaps the sudden death suffered from an accident or a heart attack? Whereas such deaths spare us months of terminal illness and suffering, they come as a shock to family and friends, who are denied the opportunity of bidding farewell. Or is good dying a slow passing away and leave-taking, which asks patients and relatives to endure much suffering in approaching death? Do those who repress their emotions die well? Or is good dying to consciously experience life, suffering, and taking leave? Is life intensified and enhanced just because we are nearing its end? (see the notion of "life embracing" in Kellehear 2014).

Good dying, for many patients, is—in their own words—to have seen and experienced much in life. Some remain in the illusionary hope of convalescence, even if they are terminally ill. Others can let go when family problems are resolved and when they know that their relatives will be supported. Good dying is "agreeing to die," replied one patient to whom I put this question. She meant that good dying involved reaching an agreement with oneself, which presupposes that body and soul are mature enough to take such a step. In these cases good dying includes final maturation and a looking back at one's life. Good dying is "experienced dying," I am often told by patients who, despite suffering considerable pain, refuse sleep-inducing medication (sedation). Instead, they prefer to go toward their death with their senses alert. One woman wished "to be present when it happened." Good dying, for other patients, is paired with their wish "to be painless and free from unbearable symptoms." They want above all symptom control and often ask for sedation at the risk of moving out of reach for their family and friends;[1] and, I would add, at the risk of interfering with an inner, spiritual process. For many patients, relatives, and professionals, good dying is, above all based on careful and sometimes meticulous decision making. Good decision making facilitates all further interventions.

How can end-of-life care ensure a good death? Recently, rapid advances have been made in palliative medicine and palliative care, in particular in terms of the humanist approach (Pellegrino 2002), structured communication (Pantilat 2009), and symptom control (Smith et al. 2012). We now also better understand the processes of maturation and individuation that occur in connection with dying (Byock 1997; Kearney 1996; Patton 2006). Physicians and caregivers take their patients' feelings seriously, as much as their helplessness (Sand 2008), their hopes, their ways of looking at the world, and their yearnings for spirituality (Balboni et al. 2010). Moreover, several therapy concepts centered on dignity, on the family, and on finding meaning have emerged (Breitbart et al. 2010; Chochinov et al. 2005; Gaeta and Price 2010; Nissim et al. 2012).

Yet notwithstanding these advances, attention remains focused on those needs of the dying that are expressed in words and that are thus more or less conscious. End-of-life care is, at present, mostly defined in terms of the rational, understanding ("seeing"), and self-determined individual. Even spiritual care is, at present, primarily focused on the expressed and conscious spiritual needs of patients (Holloway, Adamson, McSherry, and Swinton 2011:19–27). Complex processes and symptoms like "total pain," and their emotional and spiritual components (Strasser, Walker, and Bruera 2005), are readily diagnosed but largely considered only from the perspective of the ego and its ego-centered perception. By ego-centered, I do not mean egotistical but ego-based— that is, related to the human subject. For Richard Rohr (2009), the main problem of this ego-centered perspective is its dualistic thinking that "protects and pads the ego and its fear of change" (94). What we are lacking, however, is a holistic understanding of dying processes including nonverbal and symbolic signals, the unconscious dimensions, and the fundamental processes and transformations experienced by the dying. There is a lack of knowledge about patients' inner perspective and experiences. Where fear or despair prevail, where patients are suffering and distressed, when the dying process falters, then patients and their families need not only medical expertise, good communication skills, and spontaneous compassion but also therapeutic-spiritual care based on a deeper understanding of the unconscious dimension, and of dying as a transformation of perception comparable to near-death experience (Lommel 2010). We need a profound knowledge of (archetypal) spiritual processes, which happen when our everyday consciousness is transcended such as in dying processes, in spiritual experiences amid suffering, and in seeing as the mystics see (Rohr 2009). Such understanding enables a new quality of spiritual care and sometimes even guidance.

The approach needed first entails an utmost respect for the essence and personality of a particular patient. What are the verbalized needs and values of this particular patient? What are her or his deepest maybe unconscious desires or contradictions? Energies can flow or be blocked (e.g., when patients suffer from an early childhood trauma) or be neuroticized (e.g., when patients fall back into infantile communication patterns). The approach must additionally transcend the individual perspective. Thus the fundamental questions are these: What exactly is the dying process directed toward? What actually changes as the dying approach death? How do patients' inner world and values, their experiences of fear, identity, and dignity, and even their perception become transformed in nearing death?

This book provides insights into these crucial questions, that is, about "dying as a transitional process." It claims that in dying a fundamental transformation of perception occurs. Similarities in dying processes across a wide range of individuals give us the impression that dying processes are more than pure coincidence. The book is based on my experiences in accompanying more than one thousand oncological dying patients over more than fifteen years of professional practice and on research in the field, together with physicians Florian Strasser, Daniel Bueche, and Thomas Cerny (see the section "Methodology and Background Research"; Renz, Schuett Mao, Bueche, Cerny, and Strasser 2013). First published in two versions in German (Renz 2000/2008b, 2011/2015), the book offers a wider, English-speaking readership insight into the phenomenologically gathered, and hermeneutically reflected knowledge. Theoretical reasoning and arguments are illustrated by case narratives.

The book describes how patients pass through an inner threshold in consciousness and what happens before the threshold, crossing it, and beyond it (chapters 1 and 2). Mental states and sensitivity, the importance of family members, and the experiences of being, connectedness, and dignity seem to change by crossing this threshold (chapters 2, 3, and 6). For instance, distress and fears seem to increase with crossing the threshold, before transforming into serenity and trust by leaving this inner threshold behind (I refer to various descriptions of near-death experiences [NDE]: Lommel 2010; Long and Perry 2010; Parnia 2008). Many dying patients cross over and return several times, while others seem to jump over the threshold or dive into a mystery. As observers, we receive quite a lot of verbal hints as well as nonverbal signals about this mysterious transformation (Kellehear 2014; Kuhl 2002). This book is also meant to encourage professional end-of-life carers (physicians, nursing staff, therapists, pastoral caregivers, social workers), relatives, and laypersons interested in the subject. How can we empathically accompany our patients through their inner process and experiences? The insights presented here may enhance our understanding, improve our intuitions, and our spontaneous reactions at the bedside, as well as inspire discussion, further research, and education programs. Besides the verbalized needs of patients, we can learn more about their inner world by asking ourselves how they perceive and communicate. For instance, many patients who withdraw into silence or who are agitated, and whose inner life remains unknown to us, can be reached in a half-verbal or nonverbal manner after we have gained a sense of their actual experiences. They can be reached through decidedly simple questions and instructions, through symbols, or through soft monochromatic music and singing (chapters 4 and 5). Music is a means of communication between different states of consciousness (Strobel and Huppmann 1991). Music therapy, especially music-assisted relaxation, provides excellent possibilities for therapist-patient communication. In case of symbolic communication, a deeper knowledge of symbols and a symbolic, interpretive, and epistemological framework can help professionals to somehow understand patients whose experience is largely pictorial, and whose speech is at times prone to stuttering (chapter 5). All these specific aspects of dying can also be part of education programs focusing especially on enhancing sensitivity among end-of-life-care professionals.[2]

Understanding what happens spiritually and psychologically approaching death improves our therapeutic-spiritual care despite the elusive nature of the final mystery. This dimension is crucial for all professionals and relatives, in particular for therapists and pastoral caregivers. It may help in this respect to reconsider, above all in a more consolatory way, the apocalyptic and eschatological notions of various cultures and religions. This book gives several such hints. Many years of providing end-of-life care have taught me that we can neither ignore the spiritual aspects of dying processes nor focus solely on the verbalized spiritual needs of patients. The inner world of patients and their changing perceptions is strongly related to the spiritual dimension of being, and many dying patients—religious (followers of all religions) as well as agnostic—have impressive spiritual experiences.

This book differentiates between two levels, and thus twice challenges spiritual care: the individual perspective is obvious, but no less important is a hidden dimension related to human development through themes, energies, and language of transition (see figure A.3). It remains open to what degree the themes are archetypal or culturally shaped. I think that in the course of interreligious dialogue there should be an exchange about the images and metaphors communicated by the dying. We shall then gradually gain insights into intercultural similarities and differences of the inner experiences of the dying. If in this book the symbols and images stem largely from the Judeo-Christian tradition, I hope followers of other religions will explore and reflect on their own religious images as regards their inherent relevance for communication with the dying. An approach to therapeutic-spiritual care without paying attention to this meta-phorical dimension seems to me no alternative as many dying have recourse to this symbolic language in times of intense fear, struggle, and final peace.[3]

A deeper appreciation of presumably inner processes of dying patients is essential even for *adequate decision making*. Extensive wellness programs, for instance, no longer meet the changing needs of the dying for more being, tranquillity, "resonant sound," and more spirituality. Many patients are confused and disturbed by any flurry of activity and commotion. The more we understand and intuit what lies behind the symptoms, the better we can help. Such personalized end-of-life care is what I call "indication-oriented" (chapter 7; Renz et al. 2013).

Gaining a deeper sense of the inner world, states, and per-ceptions of patients may also contribute to the public debate about self-determined dying (chapter 7). Nowadays, more and more dying persons proclaim a right to die, as if they owned life and death. The term "self-determination" is misleading: self-determination is important in life to prevent an individual from becoming nothing but an object of others, power structures, and medical systems. Self-determination, however, finds its absolute limits facing nature, fate, the earth, or the divine. Dying is seen here as a natural event comparable to begetting and birth. Dying "happens" when body and soul are ready, when the whole per-son has attained a state of self-evident being and trust. In dying, as in life, there seems to be an inner alternative of human exis-tence: having versus being, fear versus trust, and power versus relationship, relatedness, spirituality (Renz 2008a). In the dying process, a profound sense of belonging and connectedness can be attained. Confronted with a patient or a family wishing a self-determined death, I always listen to their intonation: What does their voice sound like? Does their voice convey fear or rather a sense of entitlement? The French say, "C'est le ton, qui fait la musique" (It's not what you say but how you say it). And precisely this applies equally to the dying process. This book also provides some important answers concerning fear and trust that help us, for instance, in the debate about self-determined dying. I argue that fear in general depends on human consciousness and perception (chapter 3; Lommel 2010; Rohr 2009). Distress and fear transform into peace and trust—or rather into a state beyond the ego—by leaving the threshold of ego-consciousness behind. Such ego-distance occurs again and again before dying. As these concepts are so crucial for the whole book and for understanding the phenomena of fear and fearlessness, I illustrate them with three examples already voiced earlier.

In the final days of his life, Manfred Manser,[4] a man about fifty-five years old, seemed to be drifting into and out of sleep. He was unresponsive, sometimes simply lying on his deathbed with his eyes open. Suddenly, however, he flinched, contorted his face, breathed with difficulty, and once again he reentered the present. When I asked him whether he was scared of returning to the here and now because of the pain, he replied: "Exactly! In between, it is as if everything has gone. Then I feel as light as a feather."

"Fear . . . suffocating," stammered Ursula Ungerer, an elderly patient nearing death. Between outbreaks of profuse sweating, she was somnolent. Although she barely spoke anymore, she seemed to hear my words: "Beneath all fear lies trust." I assured her that she could let herself be carried by that trust. I played some music, a monochord accompanied by soft singing, which soothed her. Her breathing became more regular. She awoke one last time and told her husband that she had heard music, the music of angels. Then she drifted away—more profuse sweating—more music-assisted soothing—and she died peacefully.

———

———

Alfred Armbruster, about sixty years old, an atheist and a man of few words yet with a highly developed sensitivity for the authenticity and essence of a place or person, as well as for interpersonal relations and human communication, said after hearing me play the monochord: "How spiritual . . ." During the day, he repeatedly oscillated between two states of being. First, he was still responsive and capable of grasping these two states. In the one, he lay helplessly stricken on his bed, his face grim, contorted in obvious pain, and asked for active euthanasia. In the other, he was peaceful, looked up at his closest relatives and allowed them to look at him, until his ego once again took hold of him and he began to contemplate what dying should or should not be like. Thus his anger returned, and his pain increased. Then, at some point he regained peace. What exactly induced this peace: His daughter's love? Music? Medication? Or perhaps his tacit acceptance of his plight? A few days later, no longer responsive, Alfred Armbruster once again seemed to oscillate between two states of being: in the one, he groaned, furrowed his brow, and suddenly cried out; in the other, he was quietly composed, at peace with himself and his surroundings, his muscle tone relaxed. His daughter and I were at his bedside. Addressing this state of being, I expressed my sense of

countertransference: "Can you hear?" No reaction. "Are you hearing?" (Are you in a receptive state?) "Hhhh." His daughter and I
were impressed. "Can you hear me?" I repeated. No reaction. "Can
you hear me?" his daughter asked. Still no reaction. The question seemed to be asked the wrong way. I felt moved, somehow
touched by a sense of grace, but I swiftly dismissed this impulse:
he was an atheist and so I could not talk to him about God. And
yet the sentiment recurred. Experience has taught me that our
perceptions and needs sometimes can change approaching death,
and thus I dared to ask this dying man, paying attention to my
voice, so that I did not sound manipulative: "Is it as if you were
hearing *music*, vibrations, the divine, God?" "Yesss," he replied.
A few minutes later, he noticeably slumped back into a deep
coma. He died a few hours later.

———

So, to repeat my initial question: What, then, is good dying,
what is good death? Are we at all able to answer this question
from the perspective of our ego-based and ego-centered thoughts
and desires? And phrased thus, does this question not contradict what dying is by nature: a state beyond our control, removed
from our volition, one that is afforded the self that is willing to
die? All dying is unique, at once imposition and deliverance. Too
soon, in one way; too late, in another. Something always remains
only half-expressed or half-finished. The all-embracing nature
of death apart, dying is rupture, a breaking off. Death puts an
end to the suffering for patients while initiating new suffering
for the grieving relatives. If we are honest with ourselves, there is
no dying without suffering. But there is also no dying without a
mystery, without a religious or unreligious final process, open to
those who are looking with an inner eye and who are listening
with an inner ear. Together with a great respect for the personality

of a patient, we can become more and more sensitive, amazed, and even touched by this mystery of human existence, whether or not we refer to it as God. Can we afford to be impressed by what happens near death? Can we feel, can we recognize dignity, stage by stage, in a final essence, independently of what a patient looks like (chapters 2 and 7)? Dignified dying—in the true sense of the word—is a cultural achievement that all cultures and ethnic groups across the world must strive to preserve. The more we honor the lived life (see, e.g., dignity therapy in Chochinov et al. 2005), and the greater our knowledge about the laws and workings of life near death, the greater our astonishment. In spite of everything we know about experiences approaching death, the event of death itself and afterlife remain secret.

METHODOLOGY AND
BACKGROUND RESEARCH

This book is based on my daily work with cancer patients and their relatives (at the oncology division of St. Gallen Cantonal Hospital, one of the largest oncology and palliative care centers in Switzerland) as well as on empirical research.

- *Working method.* I provide palliative care to both inpatients and outpatients. I have developed a multidimensional approach, which offers patients psychotherapy sessions that include, among others, illness-coping strategies, dream interpretation, trauma healing, relaxation, and spiritual care. A particular interest and specialization of mine is music therapy, which involves *Klangreisen*—that is, music-assisted relaxation combined with active imagination. Our psycho-oncology team comprises three therapists (including myself), each equipped with the broad training required to provide such specialized care. We work closely with palliative care physicians and nursing staff. Weekly cross-disciplinary consultations serve to determine which patients should be recommended therapeutic-spiritual assistance. Patients may, of course, choose to accept or reject the support offered. We provide physicians and caregivers with brief updates on our assistance. Confidential issues remain strictly between patient and therapist.

• *Research methodology, data collection.* In my first years of practice, I conducted a prospective and unselected survey of dying patients (pilot study: N = 80, follow-up study: N = 600). The findings were published in the paper "Dying Is a Transition" (Renz et al. 2013). The study was based on participant observation, a method used in anthropology (Steinhauser and Barroso 2009) and ethnographic field research to study human behavioral patterns and tribal mind-sets. Participant observation permits researchers to maintain professional distance while at the same being empathically involved—that is, "participating" in events or processes. The method is also employed in the health sciences (Bluebond-Langer, Belasco, Goldman, and Belasco 2007) and is appropriate to discussing issues considered to be difficult, unconscious, or taboo for the group under study (Becker and Geer 2004). In the case of the dying, it is important that although such persons are "under observation," they are free to do as they wish: to speak, to stammer, to shout or to remain silent, to cry, or to be touched. They can share what matters to them or not, hazard or suppress the path to increasing awareness and maturation. Participant observation also facilitates registering nonverbal signals, provided they are distinct enough. The study "Dying Is a Transition" was based on my intensive accompanying of dying patients. After each therapy intervention or encounter, I recorded everything that had or had not happened. Whenever something important in the dying process occurred, I involved the physicians and nursing staff.

• *Data analysis.* The data of the pilot study were analyzed using Interpretive Phenomenological Analysis (IPA). Whereas IPA attempts to explore the internal point of view of participants, it also recognizes the active role of the researcher in interpreting the data. It is applied to data gathered by semistructured interviews or by observational methods. Small samples (three to six participants) are the rule, but an analysis of larger samples is possible. IPA is an ideographic approach to assessing relevant themes and issues, and to reflecting inherent relations and meanings without testing the data for significance or saturation (Smith, Flowers, and Larkin 2009:343). IPA has been used in metaphor research to study the unexpressed emotions of participants (Shinebourne and Smith 2010:412).

In "Dying Is a Transition," therapy records were studied by the therapist and an independent co-researcher with a background in Jungian psychology and theology. After forty reports, they discussed the emerging themes (e.g., anxiety) and subordinate themes (e.g., fear of dying/uncertainty) that each had found among the data. To better interpret the observed signals of the dying, we established a theoretical framework consisting of literature on near-death experience, intrauterine listening, and Carl Gustav Jung's studies on symbolism and archetypes. If the therapist and the co-researcher could not agree on how to interpret ambiguous nonverbal signals, they consulted a third party who had been identified in advance. The emerging themes were then discussed with the research team (Dr. Florian Strasser, Dr. Thomas Cerny, Dr. Daniel Büche, and Dr. Miriam Schütt Mao) and influenced the ongoing therapies. Later, the therapist and the co-researcher reviewed another forty reports and discussed their results until they reached consensus. Most themes were recurrent (occurring at a rate of 20% and more); one theme (trauma) and some subordinate themes were seldom but perceived as important, and they were included in the table of themes (see appendix, table).

In the follow-up study, the therapist and the co-researcher reviewed the characteristics of the themes and subthemes based on the first two hundred therapy records. Findings were consensually discussed with the study team. A final table of themes was drawn up (see figure A.1). In the end the therapist and the co-researcher independently read all six hundred records and assigned the frequency of themes, sub-themes (appendix, table, and see also the factors discussed in chapter 6). Finally, the study team discussed the resulting correlations (see figure A.1).

• *Five limitations.* (1) Our study was limited to patients with late-stage cancer. (2) Most patients were socialized in western Europe in a Christian tradition. A few patients had different cultural and religious backgrounds. An application of our findings to patients from other backgrounds is uncertain but not impossible, as these few patients show. In a further study about the spiritual experiences (Renz et al. 2015), the different religious backgrounds of patients were explored. (3) Generalizing the findings of our study might also be limited by influences of the referring physicians, nurses, and by patients' preferences. But it has to be taken into account that the study was performed in a setting with a high level of inter-professional reports, including the indication of therapeutic-spiritual support. (4) Among the eighty (pilot study) and the six hundred (follow-up study) patients cared for, only a part showed significant reactions (e.g., spiritual opening or post-transition was found among 54% in the pilot study, 51% in the follow-up study; see appendix, table). Nonetheless, it must be taken into account that a considerable number of patients may have experienced post-transition but were either unable, or too shy, or too tired to communicate. Writing about religious experience, William James (1902/2010:46) defined "ineffability" as the impossibility of conveying a spiritual experience (Arnold and Lloyd 2013:78). Thus the closer the dying move to death, the less able or willing they are to communicate about any topic. And we, as observers, are often unable to equivocally recognize their signals. For this reason, all ambiguous signals were excluded from the data, and the third analyst was consulted in case of doubt. Thus, all numbers counted have to be read as minimum numbers. The estimated number of unreported cases is high, but the large number of patients (N = 80, N = 600) still allows for making generalized statements. Further, this research generated a hypothesis but did not test it. (5) The methods also may have influenced the results (Steinhauser and Barroso 2009:338). Given that there was just one therapist, who was also the only data collector, the recorded expressions, signals, reactions, and dying processes are comparable. Conversely, the professional background of the therapist may have influenced therapies, processes, and interpretations. In spite of this limitation, four strategies may have substantially reduced these influences: the close interaction with physicians, nursing staff, and relatives concerning processes; the supervision of the therapist; the recording of data meticulously separated observation from interpretation (Finlay and Evans 2009:92); and the analyses conducted by the independent co-researcher. We refrained from involving an independent observer because participant observation requires "a naturalistic setting, with as little intrusion as possible into ongoing events" (Koenig, Back, and Crawley 2003:371).

- *Significance.* Our model of dying as a transition supplements other models of dying (e.g., Kübler-Ross 1974; Olson, Morse, and Smith 2000–2001; Wittkowski 2004), and these models complement the present approach. Elisabeth Kübler-Ross (1974) will be discussed in chapter 2. Karin Olsen and her colleagues (2000–2001) and Joachim Wittkowski (2004) developed dying models based on the grieving process. Wittkowski defined a dynamic between the factors "attachment" (*Bindung, Bindungstheorie*), meaning-making, and dying. However, these attempts generally consider dying from a so-called etic (external) rather than from an emic (internal) perspective of the dying themselves (Corr, Doka, and Kastenbaum 1999). Charles Corr (1991–1992) proposed in his model "areas of task work": physical, psychological, social, and spiritual. Robert Kastenbaum (2012:133–135) developed a "multiple-perspective approach" to dying processes. He observed that many situations that the dying have to endure are familiar to us from our own lives (e.g., experiences of helplessness), and he identified seventeen such situations. Yet all these models are mainly coping models. Factors such as shifting perception or changing consciousness (Renz et al. 2013) are not considered even if the models refer to changing emotions and awareness (Olson et al. 2000–2001; Wittkowski 2004).

The approach "Dying Is a Transition" needs further research. Additional observation studies should involve the entire palliative team (Holloway et al. 2011; Puchalski 2012). Such a study is now being conducted at the palliative units of St. Gallen and Münsterlingen hospitals, assisted by international experts from the fields of near-death experience (Pim van Lommel), theology, mysticism, and philosophy.

1

DYING AND
THE TRANSFORMATION
OF PERCEPTION

MORE THAN fifteen years of providing end-of-life care have led me to the following basic claim: *Dying is a transition*. This claim is based on the phenomenological observation of patients' states of consciousness, emotions, verbal utterances, expressed metaphors, nonverbal signals, and reactions to my interventions, and on the scientific evaluation of the material gathered from 680 patients (see introduction; appendix; Renz 2000/2008b, 2003/2010, 2011/2015; Renz, Schuett Mao, Bueche, Cerny, and Strasser 2013). The claim states:

> Dying persons undergo a transition, which consists essentially of a transformation of perception. As we approach death, all egoism and ego-centered perception (what *I* wanted, thought, felt), and all ego-based needs fade into the background. Coming to the fore is another world, state of consciousness, sensitivity, and thus another way of experiencing being, relationship, connectedness, and dignity. All this occurs irrespective of the individual's worldview and faith. Dying is a process.

EXPANDING THE CLAIM

Death as a gateway to a sphere of which we have no knowledge seems to take effect before death itself and to impel a fundamental transformation of both perception and the structure of human personality. If we observe the reactions of the dying, the mystery of death is just as alluring as it is awe-inspiring and, most of all, it is inevitable. Dying is more than physical demise and also more than spiritual-psychic decay. What emerges in approaching death is a particular kind of connectedness and being, which, as I have observed, increase.

More precisely, what Stanislav Grof and Christina Grof (1984) have called "Ich-Tod," the death of the ego, seems to precede death. The demise of the ego includes also the loss of everything attached to the ego, the conscious mind, the ego-personality, and in particular ego-centered perception (I see, I hear), ego-centered experience (I am afraid, happy, hungry), and ego-centered communication and distinctiveness (I speak, I distinguish, I want). We can barely imagine the full import of this event: the subject of our perceptions and thoughts, the governing authority, becomes insignificant. Instead, the dying person becomes immersed in a particular sphere and in perceptions of an entirely different, "holistic," non-dualistic nature (Rohr 2009). We must, however, beware of reducing the term "holistic" to the entirety of body, mind, and soul. Rather, it means the whole per se, which encompasses matter and energy as much as creator, creation, and creature. It can be conceived as another term for the divine, and it seems to manifest itself as another state of being and connectedness. This state has to be conceived as a primordial state of being (see figure A.3). This inner world does not depend on personal faith and religion (Kuhl 2002). Patients rather describe it as an acoustic environment and as a vibrational sensitivity (chapter 4).

Approaching the whole occurs not continuously but—akin to all spiritual-psychic processes—erratically, mostly in several oscillations, movements back and forth. This process sometimes leads us through crises and catastrophes (in ancient Greek, *krisis* refers to both a decisive separation and the result of a trial or a struggle—a decision that comes over one's head, a critical turn. Catastrophe, from ancient Greek *katastrophē*, means "sudden turn, overturning"; *kata*, "down, against"). Yet by no means does the dying process end there; it appears to lead us instead toward something entirely new. Even though we have no knowledge of this mystery, verbal utterances, symbols, and nonverbal signals convey to us a sense of this sphere as reported by more than 50% of patients in our study, including several nonreligious patients (see appendix, table).

More precisely, the dying seem to cross a critical, invisible threshold in consciousness. Some dying people even announce to us, not without astonishment, something indescribable: "Ohhh." Others express or acknowledge, when asked, words that point to the cognition of a transition (e.g., "passage"). Yet others experience images of descent—"I am falling"—or indeed of an apocalyptic dimension—"The dark is devouring me!" Later on, they may have a related experience: "Now light and its angels are defeating darkness." Many dying people, at some point, become entirely peaceful as if they were now at home in another world. Upon reaching this state, they seem to emanate peace or an inner glow (Fenwick and Fenwick 2008:158–159). Some are lucid, as described by the notion of "terminal lucidity" (Nahm, Greyson, and Kelly 2012). Whether alert or unaware, nothing seems to disturb their peace. This amounts to what I refer to as a spiritual opening or post-transition (chapter 2).

What occurs in such ego-distant states is related to "perception." The dimensions of time, space, and body awareness can alter so drastically that the ego can neither follow nor understand such change. Thus emerge not only experiences of simultaneity and timelessness, of overcoming spatial boundaries but also a sense of entrapment in confined or even distorted spaces as a transient state. Some experience great freedom and discover suprapersonal meaning (see also the near-death experiences reported by Lommel 2010; Long and Perry 2010; Moody 1988; Parnia 2008) while also transiting through profound existential fear or confusion. One dying patient referred to his experience as "incomprehensible!" Another dreamed that "here, you must close your eyes." That meant that she had entered a region beyond the mind, sight, and senses. Others heard utterances like "Here, you must take off your robe." From the Hebrew Bible, we know the words that Yahweh spoke to Moses in this regard: "Draw not nigh hither: put off thy shoes from off thy feet, for the place whereon thou standest is holy ground" (Exod. 3:5, KJV). A similar motif, which indicates a liminal sphere, recurs in Elijah (1 Kings 19:13): "[H]e [Elijah] wrapped his face in his mantle." Thereupon occurs the decisive self-revelation of Yahweh to Moses: "I AM THAT I AM" (Exod. 3:14). Some dying patients say "God is near."

A dying young mother, who was deeply religious and yet also sceptical, was so distressed and fearful that she could not die. We spoke with her about the experiences of dying persons and about the research findings that I had published in "Dying Is a Transition." We also spoke about "mercy," "grace," "angel of mercy," and the roots of "charity and compassion," which comes from the Hebrew word *rechem* (womb), which can be associated with *rachem* (to have compassion). She felt comforted when I told her that neither she nor her little daughter, whom she would leave behind, would fall out of the lap of God. She relaxed and then dreamed of a strange threshold that she had to cross. Curiously, on the other side of the threshold, everyone spoke English. This was all the more astonishing because her family and friends all spoke German. "What do you think that means?" she asked me. She was gripped by and yet failed to understand her experience. She was touched and became animated when I mentioned that English sometimes stands for the language of the angels for German native speakers, at least symbolically. Yes, she felt intuitively that she had been in the land of angels. And, she continued, dying could not be that awful after all.

The testimonies of many dying persons suggest that in approaching death there is an inner threshold in consciousness. Crossing this threshold, we pass into mystery, for which we have no words. Yet immediately before we reach that sphere there appears to be an anteroom. Here, the dying not only hear certain phrases and expressions, but they also behold symbols (the coming of a ship, a holy seat, a light amid darkness, a staircase resembling a stairway to heaven, and so on). These inner experiences hold a profound beauty for the dying. The symbolic experiences of the dying amount to more than a state of delirium (chapter 5). Even when nothing symbolic appears to the dying, they often experience a barely describable presence and intensity. As caregivers, we can "sense" yet never "know" such experience. We are drawn into what is in effect an experience of the absolute. Not, however, as a rigorous imperative ("You must" or "You are not allowed to") but as an encounter with something sacred. Crossing the threshold or going through the transformation of perception occurs, from the ego to being, and from self-power to connectedness. I refer to this process as "transition."

This transition and the transformation of perception appear to be the primary spiritual and emotional process in dying. Everything else (e.g., reconciliation and maturation) becomes gradually secondary. Transition and transformation occur, whether we like it or not. All deeper capacities in the dying seem invisibly focused on the transitional process and its successful outcome. The dying must go through the process rather than just remaining static. Other aspects of dying, such as bidding farewell, life review, increasing and decreasing fear, finding words for the sacred, and even several somatic symptoms seem to be reinforced temporarily because this primary process needs to be understood as a "thereupon or thereof." Then, at some point, these aspects of dying all become surprisingly secondary (chapters 5 and 6).

We cannot be too careful in formulating what constitutes dying as a transitional process. All words are metaphors, attempts to grasp the incomprehensible. And standing as we do so close to the mystery, our respect for it continues to grow. Restraint, however, is also called for in view of each person's enduring individuality. Dying is individual, just as is each person's mystery, and for this reason so too is one's very own approach to the final mystery.

2

THE THREE STAGES OF
TRANSITION AND DIGNITY

TRANSFORMATION IS MORE
THAN A PATH

Elisabeth Kübler-Ross (1974), the pioneer of end-of-life care, divided the dying process into five stages: denial, anger, bargaining, depression, and acceptance. Like the grieving process, dying, for Kübler-Ross, appears to be characterized by defiance and intense feeling until acceptance eventually occurs. The enduring value of Kübler-Ross's writings lies in her emphasizing the importance of acceptance and in summoning the courage to communicate with the dying. . And yet her view falls short of the mystery of dying. Critics (Samarel 1995; Wright and Flemons 2002) regard Kübler-Ross's approach as too linear and too pathologizing. Rather than describing what happens specifically as we approach death, Kübler-Ross speaks of the inner path that we must take until we accept dying.

In my experience, though, this challenge presents itself after every shock of diagnosis and after each stroke of fate. Going toward our inevitable death involves more than taking an inner path toward acceptance. Here transformation occurs (Kellehear 2014:204–209; Kuhl 2002:250–273). Path and transformation are two separate matters. The ego is able to cognize what a linear path is, in spite of up-and-down, back-and-forth movements. Transformation, by contrast, brings the ego up against limits that require it to stop thinking, understanding, expecting, and controlling. Thus, in transformation, the ego must surrender its governing authority. The linearity of life passes into the roundedness, simultaneity, and nonlocality of being. Transformation leads us into unsuspected dimensions. One crucial obstacle that we must overcome in the dying process consists in actually accepting transformation and deliverance. Whereas acceptance is a prerequisite for "it" to happen, it is only one aspect of the whole event. I have often observed that if patients find their inner "yes," then the process continues.

What else characterizes the dying process? The body, as the embodiment (i.e., the concentration and materialization) of this ego-centered subject, dies. And with it—and thereby initiating dying—ego-centered perception and experience wane. Dying is first characterized by a growing awareness of the end. After such realization various processes set in, including a fundamental shift in consciousness (see figure A.3).

The dying process can be divided into three phenomenologically distinct stages: *pre-transition* (before the inner threshold in consciousness), *transition itself* (across the threshold), and *post-transition* (after the threshold). Post-transition should not, however, be regarded as an "otherworld" or "afterlife" but as the most extreme state of being in this world. Many patients in our study experienced each of these stages several times.

From an observational and phenomenological perspective, we have no knowledge of such an otherworld, in spite of everything we know about dying and near-death experiences. Religions are often concerned with the concept of the otherworld or afterlife.

Because we call it "belief," we admit our lack of knowledge. In its attempt to approach the eternal mystery, this book looks in both directions to embrace contrasting aspects. On the one hand, it considers with utmost seriousness the testimonies of the dying and the metaphorical statements of religions about eschatology (theology's concern with the last things and the final destiny of the soul); on the other, it adopts the strict and modest stance of knowing nothing about the final mystery. It seems to me extremely important to maintain such final awe if we are to care respectfully for the dying. We cannot answer their final questions, let alone our own. This book does not contain statements about death per se, but it does deal with approaching death and with the "near-death sphere."

PRE-TRANSITION: BEFORE THE THRESHOLD IN CONSCIOUSNESS

Pre-transition constitutes a looking ahead, toward the threshold. On the one hand, positively experienced, impressive sensual perceptions, experiences of the here and now, and personal relationships often occur because of an enhanced intensity in this stage. On the other hand, the dying undergo negative emotions: they see the nearing "end," and fear a "demise," which is experienced even by religious persons. In the midst of suffering, many of those believers are at first disappointed by their God. Therapeutic-spiritual or pastoral care that does not eschew the question of God can help patients to arrive at a new, more adequate understanding of God.

Pre-transition is a time of *kenosis*, a time of radically giving up. The ego is deprived of all its possessions, of everything it used to be, of all identity and expectation (see figure A.3, *shaded area*). Pre-transition, among other factors, includes the reactions triggered by impending loss (e.g., denial) and the mental processes involved (e.g., the decision to consent, leave-taking, making one's last will). In this stage family processes are intense, and conflicts or distress are often resolved (catharsis). Some patients conduct a life review and let themselves be moved by unsuspected, hidden dimensions of meaning (see dignity therapy in Chochinov et al. 2005; Kuhl 2002:138–163).

Moreover, when death draws closer, day after day, hour after hour, it becomes like an avalanche crashing down a mountain or like a yawning chasm. "I am being devoured," one dying patient groaned. Later, she added, "I shall let myself be defeated by the angel," which indicated the stage of transition itself. Another dying patient felt completely lost. Later he found shelter and felt safe, which marked the stage of post-transition.

Time and again, the many symptoms suffered in pre-transition (helplessness, decreasing mobility, occasional pain, itching, thirst, nausea, etc.) are humiliating. In pre-transition, the ego remains dominant, and experience is confined to the spatial and temporal limitations of the body. Physical decline causes great suffering, fear, and shame, and patients are often unable to see beyond their strickenness. In the words of the dying, "It is getting worse every morning; I am able to do less and less"; "I am very angry at God. How can God allow such suffering?"; "I was properly dressed all my life. Now I look like a skeleton." Such moments, which may go on for hours, are also difficult for relatives to endure. Relatives are challenged to empathize with their loved one and to bear with themselves.

What Helps?

In addition to receiving the best palliative care possible, pre-transitional patients need good, bold, and careful medication as well as reliable and empathetic care. The experience-based knowledge gathered in this book helps explain why such difficult emotions and states of being are transitional realities. It also offers insight into transformation and final peace. Understanding improves care and endurance. Some patients find comparisons with near-death experiences helpful, either cognitively or because they are reminded of an extraordinary experience they had in the past (e.g., "the great light and the need I felt to love others"). Other patients find professional competence and guidance reassuring, without completely understanding. Such confidence is even more important because their life is no longer in their own hands. Completing an advance directive may help many patients feel as little exposed as possible to the workings of the medical system. Patients and their relatives need to feel that they are being taken seriously. Relatives, as observers, often feel "out of place" at the bedside of the terminally ill and the patient's physical-spiritual reality. They are not ill themselves and even less able to change anything but depend on the patient's willingness to be helped. To hear that dying is a directed process, which at some point entails a spiritual, emotional "opening" and a new perspective, helps many patients. I often explain the dying process to patients with two figures (see figures A.2 and A.3). This process constitutes an oscillation between time and timelessness, between space and nonlocality, between body awareness and out-of-body awareness, between fear and peace—all in all between two states of consciousness.

What helps patients at just this moment? In some cases, "capitulation" is a keyword; in others, "to jump off a diving board"; yet in others, a rediscovered capacity to love. Pre-transitional patients can see neither beyond nor through their state; all they can do is to accept, "to leap," to let go, and to surrender. Where this occurs with renewed openness rather than a hardening, body and soul can relax, medication will prove more effective, and an inner, spiritual process can take place.

Pre-Transition and Dignity

Dignity in suffering arises from *three* kinds of experience:

1. From the feeling of being taken seriously and being treated with dignity.
2. Dignity is an aspect of personality, which must grow from within. We can never expect all patients to possess such mental strength. Dignity in suffering stems from an inner greatness that undermines all narcissism and makes patients inwardly upright. Dignity, seen thus, is a criterion of maturity. It characterizes those persons who are able to establish an inner relationship with their suffering and situation.
3. Human dignity is first and foremost inherently inviolable.

The first aspect is easy to comprehend. The call for dignified care and treatment is heard across the world. Many palliative units, acute-care hospitals, hospices, and care homes now respond to this call. This book is a plea for what I call indication-oriented end-of-life care (chapter 7).

The second aspect, a turning inward upon oneself, is no less important. Whatever the quality of the care provided, patients will not experience dignity unless they accept the attention given, and unless they allow themselves to be touched by the affection of their relatives and caregivers. Nor will they experience dignity in suffering if they deny their transient existence. Anger and unsubmissiveness are understandable, and in order for us to remain true to ourselves in suffering, it is important that they enter into awareness. At some point, the process continues only if patients let go and risk trust. Thus experiencing dignity in suffering depends not only on a dignified setting but also on personal attitude. Dignity characterizes a person who is mature enough not to feel utterly determined by others but who is also capable of adopting a dignified inner stance in spite of adverse circumstances. Patients often tell me that they feel dignity in suffering when they can establish an inner relation to their situation, which also implies an inner distance and freedom. Amid this ever-so-slight inner and spiritual freedom, an independence from the overwhelming power of fate and a final connectedness with what we commonly refer to as "God" find expression (as discussed by the theologians Dietrich Bonhoeffer, Karl Rahner, and Edith Stein). This experience of dignity amid suffering leads to the most profound feeling of identity. Dignity is a relational term (implying reverence), but it also expresses personal autonomy, a positive attitude of saying yes even amid adverse circumstances and remaining upright and willing to endure. Only the mature person seems capable of such an attitude and of the simultaneity of relatedness and autonomy. From Jacob's wrestling with God, we are familiar with the words, "I will not let thee go, except thou bless me" (Gen. 32:26). Franz Rosenzweig (1984), a Jewish philosopher and theologian who was almost completely paralyzed, was supposed to have said, "I, who am dust and ashes, am still here" (127). One patient summed up her experience thus: "In spite of everything, I am worth it" (of being loved).

The third aspect, that human dignity is inviolable, leads us to question how dignity can be identified. Are human beings dignified by virtue of a fit and healthy ego, which determines what it wants and what it does not? Or does the notion of dignity refer to the whole person, who consists of more than a functioning ego, and more than instinctual drives and nature? According to Immanuel Kant (1724–1804; 1956) human beings possess dignity because they are moral and rational agents capable of autonomy. It is important to consider his use of the word "autonomy." Kant attributes dignity to human beings as an innermost and inalienable asset. His assertion that human beings have dignity is categorical, referring neither to empirical nor psychological facts. Human beings, for Kant, have dignity by virtue of being human. Nor does dignity, in his eyes, presuppose "self-"management and "self"-control.

In view of the millions of seriously ill people, the question of whether dignity depends on a functioning ego or whether it is instead the expression of inviolability is crucial. No longer having command over their bodies leads many patients to believe that they themselves are worthless. Misguided by the current debate, they confuse dignity with "vanity" and self-determination. They say, "I am nothing, I can't even eat without help," "I have lost my beauty, " or "I need a stick to walk and just lie around all day." I frequently hear such self-disparagement. Unfortunately, such feelings are associated increasingly with a lack of dignity of the whole person. We should not, however, cease to assume the fundamental dignity of human beings. "Yes, I am a King." These words, spoken amid suffering, represent an attitude we can learn from Jesus himself. When he was asked by Pontius Pilate: "Art thou the king of the Jews?" And Jesus said unto him, "Thou sayest" (Matt. 27:11; Mark 15:9; Luke 23:3; John 19:33–39). He was profoundly able to take a stance in his suffering. "Crown," stammered one dying patient after a spiritual experience that had evidently reassured him that he, too, possessed a secret, unfathomable dignity.

———

Lars Lechmann, a gentle cancer patient in his seventies, was tormented by recurring nighttime incontinence. He felt humiliated and—as he told me—"deprived of his male dignity." He wept and was also plagued by nightmares and hallucinations. I asked him to explain. He tossed his head, and replied, "It's always the same dream: I am running in an arena, I have to win a contest, I am running like crazy, but I don't get anywhere." In a recent dream, he had come to a gate of sorts. Standing before this entrance, he was now supposed to crawl through—well, no, actually to crawl underneath—the gate. Strangely, the gate was formed of two peacock feathers. He stood still, transfixed, and could not pass through the gateway.

———

The dream moved me. Compelled to run in an arena is contradictory, as Lars Lechmann's incontinence indicated (i.e., his body was running beyond his control). Obviously, he had to crawl underneath (the gate), which meant accepting that he was no longer in control and had lost his beauty (peacock feathers). The dream helped me empathize with this man's humiliating distress, his sense of shame at his incontinence, while at the same time he felt compelled, incessantly, to keep pace with the race being run in the arena of life. Here was a man who had once been dignified and proud, but who now had to suffer apparent indignity and to shed feathers (in this case, those of a peacock). The male peacock spreads its feathers in a gorgeous fan when it courts a female, signaling its readiness to mate; the more eyespots in the fan, the more attractive the groom. The peacock's tail and its feathers have long symbolized not only immortality but potency. My patient, his male pride dented, was challenged to find his sense of dignity amid creatureliness.

Lars Lechmann was moved by my interpretation of his dream. Although the dream eluded his rational grasp, it made intuitive sense to him. Reassured by my empathy, he contemplated the subject of dignity and the shedding of (peacock) feathers. Promptly, the nightmares stopped for several days. Something fundamental had changed: he was tired of running the rat race in the arena of life. Instead, he now acknowledged his illness and discovered a new freedom. He became drowsier. It was not yet time for the final transition prior to death, which came later unannounced and briefly. Yet, as he told me while dying, the fact that "he had practiced letting go" had helped him greatly.

As end-of-life caregivers, we are, of course, acutely aware of the pre-transitional stage, with which we automatically empathize: "If *I* were in this situation, then . . ."

TRANSITION "ITSELF": ACROSS THE THRESHOLD IN CONSCIOUSNESS

There comes a point at which we stop asking questions, and concentrate on living through the experience. In this stage, it seems that all experience culminates in an apex stage of the dying process in which things "happen" to the ego. We relax our hold, relinquishing ourselves to the utterly unknown, to move across an invisible threshold in consciousness (see figure A.3). Transition is comparable to birth, namely, in this middle stage a passing through, which takes minutes, often hours. Contrary to birth, however, transition is experienced repeatedly—because patients on their passage toward the gate of death move back and forth across this threshold. Also contrary to birth, many dying processes occur without any (noticeable) transition. A woman coming back again from the other side described her experience to her daughter: "I sailed back and forth, it was marvelous. But I yearn to stay there." The positive aspect of transition itself is experienced as a sense that "it's happening at long last." Despair, however, dominates in most cases—at least in our eyes as participant observers.

Helmut Hauser, who was about seventy years old, lay on his bed, shaking. One hand clutched the bed frame. His breathing faltered; his eyes were open. He had seen but failed to recognize me. He looked at me, startled. Did I look like a ghost to him? I introduced myself, hoping that he might recognize my voice. No change. His other hand gestured as if wanting to push aside something invisible. In a clear voice I said, "Mr. Hauser, please go on, you are in a passageway, it's awful in there. Perhaps a monster is standing in your way. Keep going, then it will open. I have seen this happen with many other patients on their way toward death." He looked at me briefly, and his body relaxed noticeably: his muscle tone softened; his hands went limp. A smile and a look of astonishment crossed his face. Then, after several minutes of silence, there followed another fright; with further encouragement from me, he regained peace. We spent two hours locked in this struggle, until he fell asleep. The next day, alert once again, he asked his wife in a sad voice why he could not die the day before in Mrs. Renz's company. Therefore, notwithstanding his incomprehension, he had recognized his own proximity both to death and to me. He died the same evening, peacefully, without going through another transition.

———

Transition is neither always quite so evident nor quite as dramatic as in Helmut Hauser's case. His example, however, illustrates what happens: all familiar structures, all laws of perception (up versus down, light versus dark, I versus you) are suspended, even lost, at least intermittently. What occurs in transition in this respect can perhaps best be described as the epitome of a process of inner movement, of transformation. Many patients are gripped by naked fear. Some of them realize, for instance, that their sense of gravity is changing, while others experience events in symbolic, visual terms: they see themselves lost or trapped between large packs of floating ice or stuck in a dragon's maw, or confronted by wild animals or by colossal machines. Sometimes they find themselves cleaning up, surrounded by cleaning utensils or by ugly spiders (chapter 5). Few of them experience apocalyptic dimensions, feel enveloped by darkness, or threatened by the "devil." By far the most frequent reactions are bodily: shuddering, profuse sweating, freezing. Such bodily experiences of our creaturely existence are what I term "primordial fear." The ego is overwhelmed and accepting at the same time.

What Helps?

In the widest sense of the term, obstetrics or the practice of midwifery helps us to assist patients in crossing the threshold. The transition demands passage, and that in itself is challenging enough. This stage involves combating symptoms, administering medication, and in some cases temporary or intermittent sedation. Patients need caregivers and relatives to be present and sensitive, particularly when patients have lost their sense of time. "Why do you leave me alone for hours?" one patient despairingly called out to his wife, who had left the room for no more than five minutes. Relatives also need support. Many are overwhelmed by the circumstances surrounding the transitional process. Some of them need instructions on how to communicate with the dying, some need to be reassured that they are entitled to intermittently leave the patient. Children, in particular, need to be spared impressions that may prove unbearable.

Nonetheless, professional end-of-life care involves more than sheer physical presence. We need to understand what actually happens. Here, in their passage toward death, dying patients need knowledgeable spiritual guides, in the true sense of the word. As professionals offering such guidance, we need to have gained a genuine understanding of transitional processes. Whenever I face suffering and struggling patients, I remind myself how such a transformation of perception might feel. How would I feel if the floor beneath my feet actually began to sway? Would I not also hold on as tightly as possible? What would it be like if I were aware of someone's presence but no longer recognized who he or she were: Would I not also be frightened, freeze, withdraw into myself, or cry out in fear? How would I feel if I were surrounded entirely by atmospheric darkness? What kind of encouragement would I need to hear to pass through the unknown, blindly? In this stage of transition, God seems to be removed, cold, and dead even for religious patients. Here pious words seem sheer mockery. Also many agnostics or atheists remark the absence of God and often use this term to state that he does not exist. When speaking to patients amid their fear, my voice is seldom gentle or sweet but assertive and firm.

On one occasion, I screamed together with a patient and fought on his behalf against his inner darkness. Yet the knowledge passed down to us from religions and folktales can help us to imagine: What is it like when both day and night have fallen into greater darkness? What was it like to be lost and abandoned in a primeval dark forest without a compass, a torch, or a map? In this regard, I find that remembering my own dreams is helpful. Archetypal images in the Bible, for instance, tell us that one day darkness will be defeated by light (Isa. 9:1, 58:10) or by a host of angels (Luke 2:13). Such statements, which need to be understood symbolically, are hardly accidental. Sometimes I mention such connections to patients who are locked in struggle. In one instance, I sought to invoke angels. In another, I just said, "It will be finished, an angel will come," and an astonished "Ahhhh" crossed the patient's lips. This happened to a middle-aged female Muslim who understood German. She was relieved and fell asleep shortly afterward. On awakening, she told me what she had just seen: the beautiful green meadow that she had come across in a previous near-death experience (in Islam, the color green is associated with the holy). She wanted to die into this meadow. I asked myself whether this woman was familiar with the myth of Mother Hulda or with a similar fairy tale.[1]

It is regrettable, I find, that secularization has cut us off from the language of the dying. Before the modern era, although even unconsciously, when people were born or died at home surrounded by their families, they possessed intuitive knowledge of how to help those undergoing transitions like childbirth and death. Although grateful for the achievements of the Enlightenment and their widespread effects, I regret the loss of such intuitive knowledge. We urgently need to find new approaches to our own culture, also to other cultures and religions characterized by an alienation from their deep roots and a split between consciousness and the unconscious (see figure A.3). Even if human development naturally comprises raising ego-consciousness, which also amounts to separation, individuals and cultures should not remain stuck in the separation longer than necessary but attain wholeness and gradually integrate aspects of the unconscious, nondualistic dimension (Rohr 2009). In the approach of C. G. Jung, the goal of a mature personality is to establish a relationship between ego and self (on the ego–self axis, see figure A.3; see also Neumann 1963). As mentioned, other religions can explore their own spiritual and archetypal materials and treasures (see introduction). Otherwise, we run the risk, particularly in Christian culture, of a splitting between reason and responsibility on the one hand, and esotericism, occultism, fundamentalism, or nihilism on the other. A new approach to the mystery of religions would help us to better understand not only the dying but also the liminal zone of life and death.

Dignity in Transition Itself

Is there dignity in failure, in the midst of existential fear? Is there dignity in complete acceptance and surrender, when events take place of their own accord and beyond our control? Is there dignity in the miserable garb of our spiritual and psychic—and often also physical—nakedness? Here, if not before, we must ask what dignity hinges on. Dignity, as an ultimate value, needs no vesture, no attributes of beauty, no outstanding accomplishments, no insignia of power. Dignity in this stage concerns our final integrity and essence. It prevails even in, and despite, the transitional process, doing so in the face of a higher truth, thereby asserting itself in dying and claiming due honor. One particular notion of dignity in transition that is rooted firmly in religion and popular belief is the image of the Last Judgment, the End of Days, the Day of Judgment. This motif is commonly believed to mark a transition to a final and eternal otherworld at the end of time. It eludes comment within the observational and phenomenological perspective of this book. From experience, however, I have found that the motif of the Last Judgment appears to many dying people during their process, even to those not seemingly dominated by a strict religious upbringing. Let me illustrate this observation with two examples.

———

Dora Dürr, a woman of about sixty, kept taking off all her clothes, compulsively removing her nightgown, underpants, everything. Was this the result of confusion? Or did this symptom point to deeper-lying causes? When I arrived at her room, her visibly embarrassed husband opened the door. Later on, alone with the naked patient and finding that I could establish rapport with the stricken Dora Dürr, I realized that I also saw before me Moses on Mount Horeb, when he removes his shoes before approaching the burning bush, recalling Eugen Drewermann's (1985:384–386) interpretation of the Moses scene: neither vesture nor shoes are needed on this sacred ground, where we come before God in our essence. I checked my impulse to share this intuition with Dora Dürr, because she seemed too confused to understand. Yet I had the image again, and eventually I ventured to tell her about it, and added, "Perhaps you feel similar to Moses: you sense the urgency of this moment, and you wish to come before God only in your essence. If this is so, then please consider, 'I am already ready,

I am pure. In my search, I am already who I am, deeply. Nothing else needs to be removed any more.'" Dora Dürr sat up and took notice. I was certain that she did not "understand"—and yet, at least for that day, her compulsion to remove her clothes had abated.

———

———

Bernhard Brunschwiler, who was in his mid-forties, was shaking. He had had a dream, but there was nothing to say. He had seen a particular chair. He was struggling for words: "The chair was standing before an altar, from which incense was rising up. I had to sit on the chair, and found that I was already naked. I was ashamed. The chair and floor shook terribly, after which there was silence. I was sitting completely upright now. A voice, no, indeed the refrain of a musical tune was telling me, 'You have done so well. You have done the right thing.' Then everything was gone." Bernhard Brunschwiler cried. He associated this dream with the biblical Last Judgment and sensed that death was near. A few days later—much sooner than his doctors had predicted—he died, peacefully. With dignity?

———

POST-TRANSITION: BEYOND THE THRESHOLD IN CONSCIOUSNESS

At some point, it is as if all fear and struggle have come to an end. Here, in post-transition, the dying enter a state of tranquility, serenity, and bliss. Qualities such as peace, deference, freedom, or indeed even true love are almost palpable. Patients are liberated from their ego-personality, imaginable as being freed "from themselves" and being freed "toward themselves," which are two faces of this emotional freedom. I have spoken to patients who came back from this state of consciousness. They told me about an atmosphere in which they were permitted to be who they are—in their essence, their very selves, their deeper identities—free of fear, greed, compulsion, and the many formative influences that had shaped their lives. One patient described this experience thus: "What I am now experiencing is not gallows humor, but a freedom from the gallows." Patients feel free and at the same time somehow connected, a connectedness with the universe, with a transcendental sphere.

They behold what we do not see. Some have visions, and many have a look of slight astonishment on their face. And even though transition is experienced several times (see figure A.2), and even though people sometimes return from the other side, all post-transitional experience is formative. "One never forgets the other side," one elderly patient told me. He was, however, unable to say more.

Most dying people pass from transition to post-transition in silence: they become still and peaceful. In her final hour, a Buddhist woman, who had been raised in Thailand, simply became quiet, almost serene, and said, "Mmm." Many dying people are simply present, emanating peace and devotion, semisomnolent, semiresponsive. Any restlessness has gone. A dying mother, whose entire body had been shuddering in transition, probably because she was the victim of a violent childhood, suddenly became calm. Her son said, "Now she is going to die." And then it happened. Some dying people begin to glow, to gesticulate, and wish to tell us what they see and hear: "So beautiful . . . ," one elderly patient, who was unable to say more, stammered. "Soon," said a young woman. "All of us," were the final, all-inclusive words uttered by an elderly woman. Frequent motifs in post-transition include flowers and just one color (blue, violet, yellow, green). "Light . . . Jesus," were the words uttered by a young, yet not particularly religious man. Another patient, a Jew, saw "a stairway, upward." Might this have been Jacob's ladder, "set up on the earth, and the top of it reached to heaven" (Gen. 28:12)? Yet the man's powerful emotion moved me. "All will be well," said a dying Muslim.

Even though post-transition sometimes lasts no more than a few minutes, at other times perhaps hours, in some rare cases days, there is an utterly different atmosphere, a state beyond time, space, and body (Lommel 2010), far away from the threshold fear and transition itself (see figure A.3). This makes such moments seem eternal.

What Helps?

When a dying person is peaceful or asleep, then relatives also begin to realize that their beloved is now in good hands, in a sphere beyond fear and pain. Some relatives manage to return to the deathbed of a loved one only when this stage has been reached. Others who were present all the time during the stage before (transition itself) now permit themselves to leave and return. I often explain to relatives that some people die only if their loved ones are gathered at their deathbed; others, however, do so only if a particular person is present (a problem child, a person to whom they feel close). Yet others pass away precisely during those ten minutes when everyone has left the room to have coffee. Whereas this is not directed against the relatives or their love, it is characteristic of people who wish to come to terms with their death on their own or who prefer to take the final step alone, also out of consideration for the pain suffered by their family and friends. Relatives greatly help their beloved depart from this world by letting go. We can never "own" our dying nor the dying of our loved ones. Dying also eludes any voyeuristically or religiously motivated curiosity. The daughter of an agnostic woman—the daughter had converted to Buddhism—wished to exert a positive influence on her mother's spiritual future (Karma, rebirth). The mother seemed tense, and her muscle tone remained hard. One night, while her daughter was fast asleep at her bedside, the mother died quietly and unnoticed. What she may have experienced and seen as insights of afterlife at the moments of passing away remained her secret.

Considering such peaceful states, it is important to explain to relatives that something mysterious and truly magnificent is occurring. I try to draw attention to the signals of the person dying and suggest how these might be interpreted. If my interpretation is consistent with their experience, it is not unusual for patients to emit a stronger signal. In such instances, many relatives "understand" precisely what is meant and are deeply touched. Such experiences as a rule remain unforgettable. Even though death amounts to a rupture for those surviving the deceased, and even though the reality of remaining behind alone is often unimaginably difficult, the moments of sharing post-transition are remembered as being beyond words. Recollecting those moments, as well as preserving and trusting that shared experience, heals the soul.

Dignity in Post-Transition

Is dignity in post-transition an issue at all? Do we not spontaneously approach such a deathbed quite reverently, as if something sacred were present in the room?

Post-transitional dignity needs to be understood as dissociation from the ego (see figure A.3). As such, it concerns the personality and the essence of the person who extends into eternity in their very own way. Essentially, we know nothing about dignity on the other side of the threshold in consciousness, at least not in terms of conventional knowledge. From the reactions of the dying, however, and from what is at times a solemn, awe-inspiring moment, we may infer that such dignity does indeed exist. Biblically speaking, such dignity touches on the divine realm, which in post-transition draws close and is almost tangibly present. This is the realm that for Christians "is not of this world." Philosophically, the awe-inspiring atmosphere that emanates from the dying in post-transition concerns the dignity that originates in the inviolability of our core essence (the third kind of dignity mentioned earlier). Theologically, this inviolability is given to humankind by God or by an absolute. Ontologically, it is about dignity in being. In post-transition, the dying are so open to life and to death, as well as to transcendence, that nothing now prevents them from accepting this final dignity.

In general, we can or cannot accept intrinsic human dignity, which derives from an ultimate source beyond ourselves rather than from within ourselves. In a personal communication (July 2001), the theologian Roman Siebenrock revealed, "We are ecstatic creatures, whose center lies beyond ourselves." We are, in the final instance, neither encapsulated within nor indeed defined solely by our egos or in terms of ourselves. We are, instead dependent and relational beings. The Latin word *personare* is a relational term and means "to sound through," to resonate or resound. Thus the Christian concept of personhood needs to be considered along these lines.

On the deathbed, these last questions of dignity and source remain a mystery. In post-transition, dying patients emanate an atmosphere of great serenity, dignity, and somehow of connectedness. Post-transition is primarily an atmospheric reality, which is not an action but a state of being, a zone of dignity.

"TOTAL SERENITY" VERSUS "TOTAL PAIN"

Current palliative care discussions frequently center on total pain. Such pain is both all-inclusive and diffuse. Today we know that what used to be regarded as emotional, social, religious, or spiritual pain (caused, for instance, by the experience of loss, retraumatization, family conflicts, or spiritual distress) can become physical and in turn exacerbate illness-induced pain. Accordingly, treatment concepts that include the spiritual dimension are now sought after. And yet the phenomenon of total pain remains largely misunderstood. We remain helpless in dealing with such pain.

Based on the insights gathered in this book, here are two observations to the discussion on total pain:

First, pain can become more intense as the dying process proceeds. Transition provokes and evokes, and brings into the twilight of semiconsciousness painful, unresolved issues. The stage of transition itself is somehow painful. Yet we should not forget that all transition is directed toward a goal, toward post-transition, toward a state beyond pain and fear—and finally toward death.

Second, pain and fear are neither the sole nor the final condition. On the contrary, total serenity occurs time and again in post-transition. Knowing this lends encouragement to many professionals, patients, and relatives, even if the dying process remains individual.

"DO ALL DYING PERSONS EXPERIENCE A FINAL PEACE?"

I am often asked this question at the end of public lectures, mostly in connection with the question about "what happens to those who suffer a sudden death." Neither of these questions can be answered conclusively from an observational or a phenomenological perspective. Some people appear to be unhappy even in dying. In such cases, I find it important to consciously think of time and space beyond the visible here and now. We have no exact knowledge of what finally happens in dying, nor in death, nor indeed in the last minutes and seconds of life. All our approaches remain interpretations. Thus the experience of a person who suffers a fatal accident, a murder, or a sudden heart attack or stroke necessarily also eludes us.

One of my most memorable experiences in this respect is a conversation with two mountaineers who survived a rockslide. Their reports come closest to an answer to whether all dying persons experience a final peace. One of the men experienced his fall as if time had become eternal, as if the past and the future had merged into simultaneity. It was, as he observed, as if "life as a whole, but also what lies beyond, had become neatly arranged in a mosaic. And as if everything had attained an inconceivable order." The second man, who was not religious, had a similar experience, not of a boundless time but of infinite space: "It was as if my body were both healthy and yet hurt by the fall, as if it now stood in an indescribable light. I was at once everywhere and nowhere. Everything was fine the way it was. I could have died, but I am alive." These experiences remind us of reports of near-death experiences (Lommel 2010; Long and Perry 2010; Parnia 2008). Do they perhaps resemble what happens in death, in the final seconds of life, in dying, irrespective of the outer impression that we leave behind?

3

WHAT IS PRIMORDIAL FEAR?

"The 'I' Dies into a 'Thou'"

INCOMPREHENSIBLE FEAR AND THE EXPERIENCE OF THE NUMINOUS

Can we empathize with that moment of dying when the ego—facing its demise and capitulating—allows itself to die? What threatens the ego as it approaches death? Whom or what does it face?

Let me explain a phenomenon that I have long suspected of epitomizing fear: primordial fear. Primordial fear already occurs in intrauterine development and then in early childhood. I have observed this fear among the dying time and again (Renz 2009). Not only is this primordial fear almost completely ignored, but it also eludes reasoning. Consequently, patients gripped by this fear feel even less understood. Suffering and paralyzed, they are unable to avoid it. Interestingly, however, they immediately understand the insights that I have gained into the nature of their distress. They seem relieved, indeed redeemed, when I share these experiences with them. Many react nonverbally, some verbally.

Feeling lost, forlorn, and forsaken is self-evident in dying (which amounts to nothing less than the demise of the ego). As I have learned from many patients, though, that is not all. There is also another aspect of fear, a "merely" atmospheric experience, which concerns *the process* of dying, of passing into darkness and the unnamed. Patients feel overwhelmed and threatened, but they do not understand themselves. They see no reason for this feeling. Here, we have to identify a phenomenon: at the heart of this fear stands an invisible experience of the numinous (see the case vignettes and note 3).

Eugen Drewermann (1987:27, 40) speaks of the primordial human fear of God. This fear, he argues, causes our fundamental distress, from which all other distress springs. And yet no one understands this term. Were I to ask people in the street or at the airport what they fear, their answers might include missing the plane, terrorism, being outcast, war, hurricanes, pain, drug addicts, mobbing, unemployment. They would, however, most certainly *not* mention any "fear of God."

I, however, claim a fear of the numinous and I speak of a Thou.[1] In so doing, I am not professing any particular religious faith. Instead, my claim comes from witnessing patients' experiences of an uttermost "atmospheric opposite." For at the threshold, when the ego is about to dissolve, it inevitably experiences this numinous Other; it does so regardless of our worldview and of our interpretation of death. I also speak of an experience of a world of vibrations, atmosphere, and sounds. Due to its changing perception as we near death, the ego at times experiences and fears the surrounding world of vibrations as an annihilating, numinous Thou. This happens regardless of whether patients have a religious affiliation or not. Numinous, here, means colossal, immeasurably large, boundless, amorphous, timeless, and thus incomprehensible. A thirteen-year-old boy explained his fear to me as follows: "Imagine what it feels like to be a flea confronted by an elephant"; an eight-year-old boy felt as if he were being devoured by an elephant. A fifty-year-old woman with late-stage cancer told me: "My incomprehensible fear is so tremendous like the Eiffel Tower in Paris. Whenever I become silent, then this fear seems to surround me. That is crazy, but I am not crazy." In moments of utter silence, the sense of a numinous world of vibrations and sounds emerges. Confronted with this world, the ego feels diminutive and utterly lost. Precisely this is the inner reality of many dying patients: The experience of the numinous Other— together with a sense of being totally naked, empty, thrown back upon oneself, forlorn, and forsaken—constitutes the "threshold experience" of approaching death. The dissolving ego encounters the incalculable One, physically understood as the sum total, of the non-ego, or a world of vibrations, atmosphere, and sounds.

> Heinrich Hutter, a man about forty years old, gradually suffered from cancer-induced tetraplegia.[2] Yet he remained keenly aware of his feelings and perceptions. He told me about his nocturnal, claustrophobic fear of large bodies of air, even though he was alone in his room and no one was either overpowering or suffocating him. He suffered outbreaks of profuse sweating and convulsions. "What could this be?" he asked. Primordial fear, I suspected, and tried to explain. He understood and nobly rephrased the thought: "Oh, I see, my perception is changing. So I suppose I can no longer clearly distinguish between details." This explained why the entirety of vibrations, the incomprehensibility of nocturnal darkness, presented an existential threat for this patient. Company soothed him. On the nights following, his partner slept in his room.

> Anita Amstutz suffered nighttime panic attacks, during which she cried out. She was unable to express her fear in words. But

she felt soothed when I told her that we subjectively experience surrounding darkness as devouring or even as obliterating. The nurses gave her a night light. Five nights later, Anita Amstutz no longer needed the light. She had evidently moved on in the dying process. She was now "immersed" and peaceful. Her perception was no longer tied to or centered on her ego.

————

————

Two days before his death, Zeno Zweifel, who was about fifty-five years old and an atheist, lay motionless on his bed, comatose. His eyes, however, were open and constantly faced the wall. Not a sound passed his lips, and his body remained impassive. His relatives and caregivers were baffled: How to explain this staring? All interventions, including mine, failed to reach Zeno Zweifel. Then, intuitively, I adopted a position similar to his, in order to expose myself to the "wall" and to my own stare. Gradually, a horror seized me: the wall was gray, its contours dissolving, and the longer I looked at the wall, the longer I beheld nothing but a terrible, atmospheric opposite. Was this how this patient felt? I said to him, "Mr. Zweifel, you must feel trapped within the mass of air confronting you. As if there were only this huge thing . . ." A piercing noise, "Ahhh," interrupted me midsentence, after which ensued a long silence and digestive noises. The latter suggested the easing of some of the tension. Encouraged by this response, I resumed our dialogue: "Mr. Zweifel, if that is *so*, then please let me tell you that whereas we find your opposite threatening, it means well with you. Let us give a name to this experience: it can be the divine or God who is looking at you, and then you will see that it or he has friendly, loving eyes."[3] "Ahhh," repeated the otherwise motionless man. His eyes were filled with tears. Did he feel understood? He responded with a silent nod. I dried his tears, remained seated for a while, and repeated my reassurance. Zeno Zweifel, I noticed, began to relax. I bid him farewell for the moment and went to see other patients. Two hours later, on my return, his eyes were closed. His face was peaceful; his muscle tone, soft. He remained in this peaceful state. Only shortly before dying did he reopen his eyes, except with a different expression, no longer frightened or paralyzed but emotionally moved and somehow transfigured. His eyes were looking and yet they looked beyond, into another sphere. They were not looking at, but through me. Zeno Zweifel died without suffering any further fear or tension.

What had helped this patient? He had needed to understand. And he had needed the encouragement that I was able to give him only out of a profound sense of empathy and from my own experience of primordial fear. Sometimes, simply encouragement helps, "to go on in the process, and all will be good in the end." Sometimes, as in the case of Zeno Zweifel, the content of the words themselves helps the dying to withdraw their projections (e.g., that the matter surrounding them is active, or that someone or something—perhaps the numinous—is intent on taking their life, "the mass of air wants to devour me"). Not uncommonly, such verbal reassurances dissipate both mental and physical suffering. Thereafter fatigue prevails. Some patients, be they religious or agnostic, are aided by recourse to a completely different conception of God, or a Supreme Being: not that of a punishing, overbearing authority, who is imagined at the same time as nice and harmless, but instead an affectionate, esteeming, and existent God, Whole, or higher power who merits our full awe and respect. Given their particular experiences of the numinous, patients have a right to hear the name commonly given to this dimension: God. Crucially, however, any mention of God ought to be nonjudgmental, nonmanipulative.

———

In the next room lay a young, panic-stricken twenty-year-old woman. Her whole body was itching, Simona tried to tell me. She was nothing but a head, she added. Simona was paralyzed from the neck down and had lost all feeling. Her mother, her father, and the nurses were helpless. "I'm going to scratch you," I told Simona and started doing precisely that. "Oh, that helps," she said. She drifted away, briefly, only for the itching to resume. Since I had known Simona for quite some time and had had several philosophical discussions with her, which had affected her physically, I moved onto this discursive level. I told her about witnessing Zeno Zweifel's distress just before coming to her room. I asked her, "Is your experience perhaps similar to his, of a great atmospheric Other that begins at the tip of your nose, where the 'I' and 'my' body end? This, you know, can cause nausea, itching, and sometimes even fear." "Yes, that's well put. But what can I do?" she asked me. I looked at Simona, intensely, and replied, "Take heart, Simona, I know from much experience that this infinite Other is actually kind and gentle, that it is actually God, to whom you enjoy praying. Try to embrace this idea." I scratched her head again. She grew calmer and seemed to better understand herself. She added, "You know, not even my nostrils belong to me anymore. That's so scary. . . . But if HE is kind . . ." No sooner had she uttered these words than she fell asleep, briefly. She was soothed. I explained to her mother and the nurse present what primordial fear is. Simona nodded once more, in agreement. She was peaceful and happy for several days. She looked up from her bed, and said, "HE—the guardian up there," had been with her.

———

Those who had shared my experience could also understand my explanation that Simona's words constituted the experience of an Other on a primary, vibrational, and acoustic level. They understood that such experience, at the limits of conscious existence, can induce fear and itching in some cases, or nausea, allergic reactions, and staring in others.

TWO ASPECTS OF
UNDERSTANDING FEAR

What is fear? Whom or what do we fear? Experience has taught me that our deepest fear is the feeling, *first, of being lost, forlorn, and forsaken*, and, *second, of being overwhelmed and threatened*, in which we fear the numinous. These are the two aspects of primordial fear, a phenomenon of which we need to raise awareness at all. By primordial fear, I mean the fear in the background, the fear lying behind and within our concrete everyday fears. This existential fear is mostly accompanied by bodily reactions. If I can name my fear, I am already coping with this underlying primordial fear. Then I am no longer gripped by fear, but I own it. Naming our fear helps to keep at bay the gruesome, the overwhelming, the inevitable.

The examples in this chapter serve to illustrate primordial fear and some of its manifestations. Such fear arises whenever the ego, aware of its creatureliness, faces a multitude of impressions that it is unable to distinguish (being lost, the first aspect of primordial fear). Precisely this inability conveys to the ego a sense of coming up against a boundless and overwhelming force, which epitomizes the second aspect of primordial fear (e.g., feeling threatened). If, on the one hand, subject-related, ego-centered perception still exists, and if patients feel their needs and fears but at the same time are no longer capable of differentiating their surroundings, then they perceive their surroundings as a numinous Other. The contours (of their surroundings) begin to dissolve. Some patients are no longer able to distinguish the wall from the painting, nor can they tell one caregiver from another, nor, in extreme cases, red from blue. And yet they are aware that something is there. They are susceptible to vibrations, atmosphere, music. In this state, they are confronted with a colossal, vibrating Other, which, as Simona put it, begins at the nostrils. Confronted with the numinous, the ego feels not only futile and lost but also overwhelmed and threatened.

It is important to speak of the numinous rather than of a void. Why would this be? Confronted with the void or with nothing, the ego would merely feel lost but not threatened. We would not understand many patients' fears and symptoms by just imagining the void. Rudolf Otto (1917/1987) has discussed the concept of the numinous in the philosophy of religion and identified its tremendous (i.e., overwhelming) and at the same time fascinating character. Dying patients discover the fascinating moment of the numinous often not in a first meeting but only in the second encounter.

Primordial fear belongs to our sense of a threshold in consciousness, not only in dying but also in ego development (both during the intrauterine stage of life and during early infancy). Primordial fear is what makes crossing that threshold so difficult. It is described by people undergoing a profound crisis. This terrifying fear lurks whenever a person descends into a crisis or crosses the threshold. At the threshold, we must (temporarily) relinquish our ego and its functions, either to die or to resume our life later under new signs. Psychology speaks of regression, which is common in suffering and illness. It amounts to more than a mere "return to childhood." Crossing the threshold, the ego is faced with reactivated childhood feelings until, eventually, it transcends them. Such liminal experiences often have a healing effect. The sphere lying behind the threshold carries great healing potential.

In terms of folktale imagery, in regression and illness those who cross the threshold spend a timeless period in the realm of the Great Mother, either in the underworld of Mother Hulda (see chapter 2, note 1) or in several other folktales about a taboo in a forbidden room (Riedel 1978). Heroes and heroines find refuge, for example, in the cottage of a wise woman with a spinning wheel (e.g., "The Goose-Girl at the Well").[4] In "The Girl Without Hands,"[5] a folktale collected by the Brothers Grimm, a young, armless woman comes to the house of an angel bearing the strange sign "Here anyone can live free."

Archetypal images in dreams and imaginations such as mothers or angels of either darkness or light lead us through regression to worldly wisdom and to a sense of meaning and purpose. Thus, these are initiation experiences and have been the subject of ethnography. For example, Arnold van Gennep (1909) studied rites of passage and divided them into three phases: pre-liminality, liminality, and post-liminality. Victor Turner (1969) later took up this idea and focused on the liminal stage. He defined this stage as a state "betwixt and between the positions assigned and arrayed by law, custom, convention, and ceremonial" (95). The threshold experience is part of every transition and reconnects us with archetypal dimensions and their regenerative and healing powers.

Folktales and the narratives in the Bible and maybe in scriptures of other religions teach us in images and metaphors what constitutes our fear of the threshold, and what shapes and dangers this fear commands in confronting us. Common themes include being lost, being devoured, falling into a bottomless abyss, or being abandoned to dark powers or wild animals: in the Bible, Jonah, fleeing from the presence of the LORD, is pitched overboard during a storm at sea and swallowed by a whale. Hansel and Gretel, in the Brothers Grimm tale, are left in a dark wood and captured by a child-devouring witch. In the ancient Greek folktale of Amor and Psyche, the daughter of a king is stranded on a high mountain and left to perish alone (Neumann 1983).

From dream symbolism and the experiences of the seriously ill and dying, we know that folktales are more than merely "fairy tales," more than invented narratives. In dreams, the dream-ego is also threatened, apathetic, sick, famished, overwhelmed, or almost killed. Some dreams are about being devoured by the night, or a yawning chasm, or—reflecting our civilization—by colossal machines. Some dreamers feel caught between magic and curses, or frozen in an "ice cave," or lost in a desert. The symbolic experiences of the dying are similar (chapter 5).

In summary, whether experienced in life or near death, we must identify the two principal aspects of primordial fear:

> First, the fear of being abandoned, lost, forlorn and forsaken, which in effect means disconnected: typically experienced as the fear of being alone or lost in a desert, as the fear of freezing or starving, and as the fear of the void. Lack of love, life, and nurture (the "too little"). Too few vibrations. Monotony and emptiness. Creatureliness and nakedness. **This first aspect concerns the perception of self.**
>
> Second, the fear of being overwhelmed and threatened, the fear of the numinous: the experience of existential threat resulting from too little space, or too much heat, or facing unknown powers (animals, witches, machines), or being exposed to the forces of nature. This second aspect of fear epitomizes the experience of the Other. Feeling cramped and constricted amidst "the too

much" of impressions and violence. Too many vibrations. Noise and plethora. (Renz 2009:146) **This second aspect concerns the perception of the other.**

Both aspects afflict us existentially. In dying, the process brings the ego to the point of capitulation. Patients experience primordial fear both before and in capitulation, mostly in an unconscious manner. The demise of the futile and lost ego goes along with the experience of the numinous, which is once again tremendous and archaic, as it was in the early childhood. The dying patients see nothing but "the end." Crossing the threshold in consciousness, they are paralyzed and their perception suspended. The contours of their surroundings become blurred (which signals the transformation of perception). Subjectively, the end, the blackness, the wholeness, or the otherness overwhelms the ego. The sum total of vibrations becomes a crushing body of air. Nocturnal darkness expand, sounds and movements become threatening or turn into devouring animals, giants, or machines. Noises or movements are experienced as malicious and active instead of matter per se.

And why is this experience also connected with forlorness? Because the ego—in dying—is left to itself, naked and nothing, no more than a "thing," without any potency, capacity, mobility, and beauty. At this point, the post-transitional state of peace and connectedness is still far away.

FEAR IS INHERENTLY EGO-BOUND

Fear in its archaic form happens, unsolicited, unbidden, as one or several bodily reactions—shaking, shuddering, sweating, freezing. It is one of our profoundest emotions that seizes or indeed even overpowers us. It is fundamentally associated with our experience of subjecthood. Only if we have a sense of self with its bodily and sensory perception do we feel fear. In a developmental perspective, fear emerges during the earliest stage of the development of human consciousness, ontogenetically and phylogenetically. Primordial fear is an older, earlier form of fear, which is also experienced by embryos, fetuses, children, and animals. They all begin at some point to react as subjects. They are all in need of themselves, even unconsciously, much more than the world of plants, and in contradiction to many descriptions of near-death experiences. Fear or anxiety occurs only in a state of at least minimal subjecthood. Fear is ego-bound and has never concerned us beyond our ego-centered experience. Although we are barely able to make sense of this statement, its validity becomes evident whenever the dying describe or confirm experiences of happiness or light, timelessness and peace, when—after an attack of fear or pain—they descend into another (post-transitional) mode of perception and being.

A dying monk, immediately after suffering intense cold and despair, became serene. His last words to his confrères, and thus to this world, were, "God is quite different!" The dying process had evidently taken him to a sphere that lay beyond fear.

In dying as in life, we may unexpectedly feel deeply safe and secure. Such an experience of a fearless existence is offered to us as a gift, sometimes described as being close to God, sometimes explained just as an altered state of being. It happens, for instance, after music-assisted relaxation, during an inner experience, when dying patients see angels, the starry heavens, or signal astonishment at a peculiar freedom and all-embracing connectedness. Such experiences convey a sense of bliss or emotional security, in general a state far removed from fear. We have similar reports from people with near-death experiences, or with "sacred" dreams.

Fear is a part of life but not necessarily a part of being. Fear belongs to ego-centered existence but not necessarily to a state of being connected to a greater whole, God, or a higher power. Patients have many "out-of-fear" experiences (see the section "Post-Transition" in chapter 2; figure A.3; Lommel 2010).

DYING PROCESSES ARE DIRECTIONAL: FROM THE EXPERIENCE OF THE OTHER TO SPIRITUAL OPENING

The case vignettes examined so far have illustrated the experience of the numinous Other from a phenomenological perspective. In this section I approach this experience based on my concept of the human being and its developing consciousness. My basic assumption is that from a spiritual viewpoint, we are part of and participate in a larger whole. We can perhaps best imagine such a state as a fundamentally different mode of perception, as a "greater" condition beyond rational understanding. The reports on record from near-death experiences, and from post-coma patients go in this direction. In mythological terms, this state is akin to paradise.

Given such an uttermost participation in what could be said to be a primal state of humanity, then all individuation or the process of our becoming an ego (see figure 3.A, *upward-pointing arrow*), and more fundamentally a subject, also means taking leave and becoming lost. Not, however, as the suffering of punishment, as the biblical myth of Creation about the expulsion from paradise suggests. Rather, the mythological loss of paradise occurs due to a transformation of perception and marks a pivotal experience in the early development of human consciousness. To the extent that in the womb the embryo or fetus, and to the extent that after birth the baby experiences life as an ego—hearing, feeling, drinking, and so on from its specific ego-centered viewpoint, and on its own terms—perception is selective and governed by subjectivity. For instance, the world of intrauterine sounds, which we know is full of commotion, is filtered out. This has to be seen as an achievement in early human brain development. As a result of such selections, the developing person no longer feels part of the whole. Individuation starts with altering perception—and so does dying but in the opposite direction.

Dying processes are directional. They sometimes lead the dying through the described intense moments of primordial fear into a fundamental trust, through stupor to softening. These processes sometimes lead the dying through the panic of falling out of everything (i.e., a profound sense of failure) into a deeper sense of "falling into" and feeling cared for. The dying enter into post-transition, also called "spiritual opening." What we see as observers is merely a change, especially a changing atmosphere: "it" opens. Precisely this opening is linked to spirituality: a highly spiritual experience situated between the human world and a transcendent sphere (the word "spirit" comes from the Latin *spiritus* and the Greek *pneumatikos*. The Greek verb *pneó* means "to breathe, to blow, wind").

Theologically speaking, we die from our ego-centered being— through this difficult experience of the numinous (which our concepts of God have obscured from time immemorial)—into God as the whole. Karl Rahner (2000) said on his eightieth birthday that "the immense and silent void we experience as death is in reality filled with the primordial mystery we call God . . ." (15).

Phenomenologically speaking, we have many reactions such as astonishment, the change from agitation to peace, combined with uttering particular words ("light," "I'm free," "flowers," "crown," "ceremony").

Ontologically interpreted, in transition we seem to experience the Other, and we die into an atmospheric Thou and enter into a new mode of perception.

The death of the ego leads us through our very own primordial fear. There is no escape from the inevitable. Precisely this experience of going through makes transition a *transition* (see figure A.3, *shaded area*). Of course, neuroscientific approaches can explain parts of such processes (e.g., Bruno, Ledoux, and Laureys 2009), but not the process nor the mystery as a whole. Following Moses (Exod. 3:14), I would formulate the *mystical perspective* thus: the ego, the "I," dies into an I AM THAT I AM.

THE NEED TO "LET GO" AND TO "FIND" RESOLUTION AND REDEMPTION

Does the previous discussion of our primordial fear (of forsakenness and of the numinous) exhaust the manifold types of human fear and the distress suffered by the dying from time to time? Does explaining primordial fear suffice to account for the human condition? Perhaps not. We need also to discuss where fear prevails indirectly in our lives, which formative influences spring from this primordial fear, and which patterns of reaction enter into play. Consideration must also be given to whether someone has more or less "inner drive" (energetic constitution), and what kind of particular cultural imprinting holds for them—for instance, the reflexes of ownership and power, and the tendency toward lethargy. The dying must let go of all these modes and patterns as well as many influences of civilization and religion. They must allow self-enclosure, narcissism, greed, possessiveness, egoism, competitiveness, and domineering behavior to dissolve. In dying we must let go of all hardening in the ego, all defensive reactions, the inner "no," and the structure of desire, all of which go back to our primordial reflexes and instincts (chapter 7). Dying means freeing ourselves, so that we may be free to be only and essentially ourselves.

———

On his deathbed Erich Ehrbar, who had spent his life adhering to social conventions, said to his wife: "I have never felt so free. It is as if a great weight, indeed even all family and social baggage, have been taken off my shoulders. As if I only have to be Erich, now I am just that."

———

Letting go of fear and imprinting amounts to existential freedom. As dying patients signalize, their finding has to do with freedom and peace, with a greater relatedness and all-embracing connectedness, and at last with spirituality and being. Not only do we go toward our dying, but dying—and the mystery behind it—also comes toward us. We act, and we are acted upon.

4

OTHER HEARING

Beyond Space and Time

SOUND IS SPACE, RHYTHM IS TIME

Many dying persons can still hear, even if they no longer seem to visibly respond to the external world. Somnolent patients also respond to acoustic signals, in particular to music (Schroeder-Sheker 2007). Neurobiological research shows that music has positive effects on pain, fear, and depression (Archie, Bruera, and Cohen 2013).

Music is the medium farthest removed from consciousness. It combines sound and rhythm, tone (sound material), and time (intonation and dynamics). Sound is *space* made audible. Sound is *being* made audible. Rhythm is time that is able to be experienced and is the most original and ultimate experience of time: prehistoric humans oriented themselves to rhythms, the embryo and fetus to the mother's heartbeat (Tomatis 1987; van Leeuwen et al. 2009), the infant to the breast-feeding rhythm. For dying persons, rhythms become increasingly less important. I experienced that even in former rock musicians. Instead, the tonal "dimension of being" becomes ever more important, as abundance and plethora, emptiness and monotony, sometimes first as the numinous Other and then as the experience of being at peace (post-transitional musical sensitivity). I have spoken elsewhere of the changing experience of music (Renz 2000/2008b:59–60, 2009).

Here, the term "music" must be taken as the inclusive sound-silence continuum for a dying person, the entire tonal and rhythmic plane of stillness and noise, vocal pitch, and repressed and unspoken words, the inaudible sounds of the plant world, and Mozart played in a patient's room, the clattering noise of a CD player. Formally framed music is only part of this world of sounds. It is this whole world of sound and the sum of vibrations that reach the dying, which in effect amounts to their world. The dying are either related to this world, or in complete accordance with it (*unio mystica*), or helplessly exposed to it. As their mobility declines, they are increasingly less capable of changing the intensity or monotony of the surrounding vibrations. This means that the dying depend on our understanding and empathetic listening to positively influence this world of sounds and vibrations. For instance, how might the patient feel the calm of birdsong? Or how might he frame the constant, colossal ticking of a clock (perhaps as the noise of a beast clearing its throat in fits and starts)? What might an immobilized patient make of motorcycles or car brakes screeching in the background? Such patients often can no longer distinguish outdoors from indoors but only sense the world as noise. What about a ghostly, almost "devouring" silence at night? Either of these musical extremes—noise (too many vibrations) on the one hand, and monotony (too few vibrations) on the other—may make breathing difficult for the dying, even though "nothing" (nothing object-like, nothing visible) is present. Whether the dying like it or not, vibrations are either sustaining or threatening: they are either what the dying can open toward completely or must brace themselves against, closing themselves off imperceptibly. Tension, pain, and feelings of helplessness grow as a result of such experience.

Our sense of time also changes as we approach death, at first with difficult and, later, with liberating effects: "Why does nobody come, I pressed the button?" "Why did you leave me alone for hours?" one man screams at his wife, who had briefly left the room to catch some fresh air. Once we lose our sense of time, sheer waiting—be it for as little as five minutes in real-world terms—turns into a feeling of eternal forsakenness. As with infants, care—understanding, affectionate care—should be given promptly. At such moments, it is useless to account for one's own distress: the dying, just as infants, would not understand anyway. Rather, we need to do our utmost to help and to understand that the dying are beyond comprehending. For example, on impulse one woman affectionately said to her terminally ill husband: "Yes, of course, you are angry at me. So would I be if I were you." But she did not have to justify leaving his bedside for ten minutes.

Why do the dying have no sense of time? What the infant does not yet know—for instance, how long an hour is—the dying no longer know. This often applies to the seriously ill before they enter into the dying process. Whereas embryos, fetuses, and infants first orient themselves to rhythms of the mother's heartbeat (van Leeuwen et al. 2009), breast-feeding, day and night, the seriously ill and the dying orient themselves to rhythms and regular events so as to maintain something of the ego's sense of time: the rhythms of caregiving, eating, the rounds of day and night, of visiting, and so forth. At some point, however, the dying lose such orientation, so that any outer change is frightening. Suddenly those at their bedside appear to be black shadows. Suddenly their surroundings are either dark or light. Suddenly there is pain, even though it has long since announced itself. Such abrupt awareness is inherent in all changing perceptions. Suddenly, familiar points of orientation are lost, while a new world and mode of being have not yet arrived. On the contrary, at this stage the dying see neither through nor "beyond, to the other side." The transition from the ego to being passes through crises. Transition is rough, spasmodic, a continuous—and challenging—back-and-forth.

> Pierre Pavarotti, a middle-aged man, told me: "I can no longer think straight about my life. I was always keen to see the bigger picture, but not even that is possible now. Actually, I can only decide against being afraid and trusting you [physicians, nurses, caregivers, relatives]."

Caregivers need to take into account that the dying lose their sense of time. We can never be sure if the dying patient is present in the ego, and in the here and now, or not. Does he still know what five minutes are (pre-transition) or does he feel lost and caught in an intermediate stage of eternally, unbearably expanding time (transition itself)? Or has he even reached peaceful post-transition, where time has become superfluous? Whereas these questions remain unresolved, owing to their very nature, raising them alerts us to being keenly aware of the dying persons's changing needs.

THE AUDITIVE SENSITIVITY
OF THE DYING

One of the fundamental points of this book is that the dying can hear. By this, I mean something more comprehensive than "active listening" and intact recognition. Time and again, I have encountered dying people who, although somnolent, could "hear" and respond to words, even sentences, uttered in their presence.

Perhaps some of them were waiting for a liberating message—for instance, amid difficult family problems. Whereas previously they may not have responded to anything or anyone for hours, as soon as they hear the message of peace that they were waiting for, or as soon as their long-lost child comes to their bedside, they are once again responsive and even try to respond (chapter 6). Then a directed listening of sorts occurs, in order to purposefully filter a message from the surrounding noise.

"Being in the hearing state," beyond directed hearing, means to be vibrationally present, a state expressing uttermost relatedness beyond ego-centeredness and narcissism; pure openness, beyond all hardening (Rohr 2009). This special sensitivity of the dying is a mode of being. And further, I speak of two different states of consciousness: our everyday ego-centered consciousness, and—across the threshold—a fundamentally other, ego-distant consciousness characterized by spiritual connectedness (see figure A.3). When patients are in a state of hearing sensitivity, they are near the threshold of consciousness (see figure A.3, *shaded area* and post-transitional zone).

Yet such hearing is not unproblematic, because "betwixt and between" (Turner 1969:95) the two states of consciousness emerges a heightened sensitivity to disharmony, stress, unresolved family tensions. The dying are highly dependent, in the first instance exposed to a multitude of impressions. Pre-transition and, even more, transition itself are states of uttermost dependency, but then, in post-transition, patients mostly pass into magnificent connectedness, freedom, and peace beyond any restraining influences. "So beautiful . . . ," stammered one man, deeply moved by something only he could see while a jackhammer roared next door. Nothing, nobody, could disturb his inner peace. Others experience a painless state beyond any distress or disquiet. "I am surprised to be so cheerful. I am no longer afraid," a dying tetraplegic patient explained, in a slow and flat voice. His hearing was at the same time his inner seeing: He saw the color yellow.

In light of what we know today about intrauterine hearing or about coma patients and near-death experiences, it is hardly surprising that the dying can hear. I am referring to the auditive phases of life, which always occur in liminal states, on the verge of transcendence, and thus in close proximity to the threshold in consciousness and its crossing discussed earlier (Strobel and Huppmann 1991). Auditive phases include intrauterine development and infancy (individuation), deep regressions during severe illness and crises, comas, and dying. Already hearing in the womb, we emerge upon our individual paths toward attaining self-awareness; at the end of life we pass away into an uttermost Thou, hearing. Transition, then—and this is my essential claim—is essentially acoustic. It is helpful to be aware of this specific hearing sensitivity of the dying. In my own case, besides my training as a music therapist, personal experiences, such as being bedridden for months with a serious illness or recovering from several accidents, concussion, and whiplash, have taught me just as much about the hearing and the specific spiritual sensitivity of the dying.

Experience has also taught me that we cannot rationally acquire such sensitivity for the dying. Instead, we need to listen intently, remaining alert to the language coming from the depths of our soul. Music-assisted relaxation and imagination can raise our awareness. For this reason, I always include both forms of practice in my training programs in addition to teaching the theoretical fundamentals. I also encourage participants to listen to their own voices and intonations, so as to detect underlying intentions and uncertainties for whatever I say will reach patients as music. If I am unable or unwilling to listen to myself, neither will my patients. Hearing is also feeling; going in search of our unconscious makes us authentic. I also aim to remain genuinely concerned and compassionate, allowing for my own limits. Not only the dying undergo a process but also do end-of-life care-givers. When recruiting palliative care staff, close attention must be given to various criteria, including professional expertise and interpersonal skills in addition to compassion, hearing sensitivity, and a familiarity with suffering.

5

METAPHORS OF TRANSITION

THE ANALOGICAL AND SYMBOLIC EXPERIENCE OF THE DYING

———

Martha Meier, an elderly woman, clutched the bed frame and screamed, "Help, I am falling!" Beneath her opened what she perceived to be a gaping chasm. In other words, her sense of gravity was changing. Symptomatic of her shifting perception was her subjective experience of falling—of falling out, of falling into, of falling through.

———

———

Rudolf Rast, an elderly man, cried out, "Up, up, up. Säntis [the name of a mountain near his former home in Switzerland]." His hands made an urging forward movement. Inwardly, Rudolf Rast was hiking up Mount Säntis. Then he "came up against a brick wall," the bridge across a deep abyss was broken. "Upward!": I encouraged him and reached out with my hands to offer him a bridge to cross. Then I explained to him about the mountain

he was climbing or about the bridge and the abyss he was crossing; these metaphors signified that he was approaching death and
the threshold of consciousness. I reassured him that he was moving in the right direction. I encouraged him to climb and then to
cross an inner threshold. Rudolf Rast pulled my hand, firmer and
firmer, before slumping back into his bed, drowsily. The motif did
not recur. Had it been understood?

———

Are dying patients delirious? In my experience, whereas the
term "delirium" may be appropriate in isolated cases, it does not
apply to the majority of dying persons undergoing transition.
With regard to the dying, I prefer to speak of terminal communication and symbolic language. The dying no longer think or
experience in rational-logical terms. Yet this does not mean that
they are illogical or confused. Their communication, instead, is
analogical and metaphorical. This distinction is crucial for a dignified approach to the dying. "Delirious" often means incomprehensible and without dignity. By contrast, the notion of symbolic
language assigns meaning to the utterances and communication of the dying and affords us an opportunity to empathize
with them. Symbols are never coincidental. Instead, they represent energy, a particular theme, the pressure to change. Thus
in symbolic expression we discover patterns, repetitions, utterances that express both a person's essence and his distress. Such
communication offers practitioners the opportunity to respond
on a symbolic level. When a patient sees spiders and spider-
webs, for example, and feels a housecleaning urge, rather than
saying, "Everything is clean here, the cleaning lady comes every
morning," I query the patient further. Who knows, perhaps the
remark refers to spiritual-psychic cleansing. Or it may point to

the fear of feeling trapped in a web (of personal relations). Or the expression perhaps indicates the mysterious power or wisdom that constellates itself just now, before dying, and which overcomes the existing order. In other cases, when a patient perceives a struggle with darkness, not only do I switch on the room light but I also join in the search for the *inner* light. I might ask the patient about angels and recall a finally victorious apocalyptic struggle. Especially in cases of struggle, it is important to mention images in scriptures such as apocalyptic metaphors and the inherent logic of a victory. Otherwise patients may be caught in an impasse (dream consciousness) independent of their religious or nonreligious attitude. As noted in the introduction, members of other religions are invited to explore their own religious material related to the dying process. Whether such images have to be taken as facts (e.g., prophecy of afterlife) or as a metaphorical world, remains open. Research has to carefully distinguish between observation and interpretation.

Rather than pathologizing patients, I endeavor to regard their condition, their strange manners of expression, their occasionally "impossible" reactions, as "normal under the circumstances." Would I too not be affected similarly by the exceptional circumstances? Would I not also scream, whine, freeze, or recount my visions, regardless of whether those gathered at my bedside speak my language or not?

What Helps?

Dealing appropriately with the symbolic experiences of the dying requires a particular sensitivity, acumen, and perspicacity.

To begin with, the meaning of an utterance, a gesture, or a scream escapes me. And thus I set out, tentatively, on my search for meaning.

Indispensable assistance in this search comes from a knowledge of symbolic connections. A dictionary or encyclopedia of symbols apart, I also find C. G. Jung's dream interpretation on the subjective level useful. Jung considers the figures appearing in dreams to be a part of ourselves. Thus, the dream image of a famished dog might reflect the starving, hungry aspect of one's own soul. Or the dream of a damaged car may stand for "feeling like a wreck." Or, as in the folktale of Mother Hulda, a Gold Mary and a Pitch Mary may appear in a dream as two opposite parts of one's own self (see chapter 2, note 1). Seeking to understand the symbolic language of patients, I pay close attention in particular to recurrent motifs (e.g., ship, mountain, knapsack) and to forms of energy (e.g., movements, colors, good versus evil). For instance, when a dying person faces a mountain, either in a dream or in a waking state, and remains standing before this obstacle, shivering but also deeply moved, I might ask whether they feel as if she had a "mountain to climb." It is as if she could no longer see "beyond"—that is, beyond all her difficulties. Or I would consider my own associations and amplifications and ask myself whether perhaps the patient sees a holy mountain, where, for example, Moses worshipped and encountered God face-to-face. I feel my way forward, slowly, discarding impulses and discovering new ones. What I neither dare nor permit myself, out of respect for those in my care, is to speak of coincidence or meaninglessness. Failing to understand the signals of the dying from our external vantage point under no circumstances means that they are unintelligible. Nor does failing to fathom an utterance or gesture, or the language of a bodily symptom, suggest that such expressions or suffering have no meaning. On the contrary, incomprehension reveals one's own limitations. The inner and outer perspective are two distinct matters.

IMPORTANT SYMBOLS IN PRE-TRANSITION

The following list of some frequent symbols and their possible meanings is meant to provide orientation, and the symbols are assigned to the three stages of the dying process: pre-transition, transition itself, and post-transition (see also Renz 2009:80–81).

Symbolic experience in pre-transition occurs seldom at this stage because the ego still commands all its functions and represses what later comes to the surface, beyond our control. Sometimes the dying surround themselves with a symbolic protective wall. Processes such as letting go and acceptance, leave-taking, resolving difficulties, fear, and struggle occur in terms of analogies and on a semiconscious level. Thus patients are confronted neither with humiliation or shame nor with admitted guilt. The narcissistic wound that comes along with diminished vitality and physical beauty can thus better be kept at a distance. Dying is our greatest narcissistic wound. There are also other reasons for symbolic experiences, such as brain metastases, and a special sensitivity and strong personality that enable us to participate in the darkest sides and mysteries of life and destiny. Time and again I have observed that highly impressive personalities, in approaching death, attempt to take their ultimate steps toward consciousness-raising. Their inner path, which probably never completely rises consciously to the fore, leads them to contemplate archetypal themes or themes in the history of humanity. Intuition often encompasses what lies beyond our grasp, beyond comprehension. Entering the depths is both an honor and an imposition. Can we assist the dying and their relatives in this respect? Can we understand their images? What exactly do the dying see in pre-transition?

1. Dying patients find themselves standing by the sea and falling into the water; they lose their way in the forest; they stumble around in the fog, in swamps, in the undergrowth; they get lost in the desert. Such scenes represent an inner approach to primordial fear and states of being, which the dying need to pass through. The fall into a bottomless pit is imminent.

2. The dying encounter an obstacle, a mountain, or a tunnel that is still closed; they are trapped in a water pipe or on a construction site, which suggests a (re)building of the soul.

3. They face a difficult journey or mountain hike. Obstacles prevent their departure: a flight has been cancelled, the car will not move, there is no food, or other circumstances keep them from leaving. Sometimes, they see before them a vehicle, a "bicycle-car," a "silver subway train." They need to make a crossing. All familiar patterns of life no longer suit the task. At times this process occurs under pressure. Yet if caregivers understand the symbols, such situations hold out a promising atmosphere, a silver lining.

4. They see the broken wing of a bird. Bound to its "last nest," the creature envisions its demise. In Greek mythology, a phoenix (literally, an "ash-like bird") promises resurrection from its own ashes. The image forebodes change.

5. Dirt and soul cleansing.

6. The dying feel naked, and ashamed. Their clothes may have been stolen; their festive dress, mislaid. Some are panicky about

arriving too late because they are not yet "ready" for the feast. Matters are not as they should be.

7. Gargantuan animals, giant spiders, monsters, dragons, wolves, the dark sinister stranger: these phenomena foreshadow a numinous experience. As yet the dying are still in pre-transition, but the transitional process is near. Such symbols stand for a vibrational world that has become threatening. The images also include repressed biographical contents (such as traumas experienced long ago).

8. Defunct wiring presents itself but at the same time the dying perceive another sort of electricity plant. Old associations and ties are past, new "connections" not yet found, pointing to the energetic dimension.

9. Eyes or a giant eye symbolize the experience of being looked at by and within the numinous. This sensation sometimes relates to a heightened sense of awareness (paranoia). Usually, however, the symbolic eye "wants" to kindly "touch" us and establish a relationship.

10. Black and gray: the ego sees neither beyond nor through.

11. A curse, the devil, black beside white (such as a black-and-white power line as an energetic statement). Such images capture the impending struggle between good and evil in terms of the repressed, the tabooed, the shadowed. Even though we know nothing about such dimensions, there are patients who report such images and who intuit the existence of such powers, which need to be understood.

In pre-transition, patients need to be encouraged to let themselves fall, to jump, to accept, to let matters take their course, to pass through. Some benefit from a protective ritual or blessing offered, others from being encouraged to continue step by step.

IMPORTANT SYMBOLS IN TRANSITION ITSELF

In this state, everything is changing. Patients are no longer "looking" or waiting, as in pre-transition. They are betwixt and between, as it were. Here are some frequent symbolic sequences:

1. The sea or a chasm opens (sometimes symbolized by a dragon). The fall takes place. Primordial fears and threatening primordial states are unleashed. The dying feel lost in a forest, in fog, or in a desert. Everything is dark, wet, cold, or hot. The ego surrenders, is defenseless, and falls. Everything, the sum total of particles, descends on them . . . until, at some point, the mass of individual particles are organized into a beautiful color. The gorge, chasm, or dungeon in which patients are trapped suddenly provides some little space to stand. Movement or change may occur.

2. The dying are caught in a water pipe; inside the tunnel, space is dark, surrounded by mountains, and confined. The construction site expands, an explosion, a deafening noise. Suddenly, they see a passage.

3. The dying set off on their journey. There is a storm. Their plane crashes, re-emerges from the debris, and continues its flight. Obstacles (animals, walls) grow ever larger and momentous, until suddenly they vanish. Equipment is now superfluous.

4. Paralysis spreads. In transition, the symbol of the phoenix now stands for "a cloud of ash and smoke." Confinement and paralysis become like a cocoon. Patients feel "trapped, buried alive." This image suggests change through pupation: from the caterpillar to the butterfly.

5. Dirt and soul cleansing are now fully under way. Sometimes, patients are restless, itching, vomiting, and so on.

6.   Freezing and shivering (as a consequence of inner nakedness or as expressing a total sense of loss). Heat and perspiration.
Sometimes, the dying must walk through a fire. Nakedness is a
gateway to the underworld, to soul cleansing, and to becoming
whole. What becomes evident at this stage is who we are and
what we were in life. Nakedness, such as compulsive undressing,
might also indicate that the time has come to strip down—that
is, to risk an encounter with the sacred in our very essence: from
semblance to being.

7.   Overwhelmed by monsters, as an epitome of helplessness,
confinement, nausea, allergy, anxiety. Some dying behold their
dissolution into individual molecules, others simply experience
transition. Sometimes protective rituals or blessing helps. It is
not yet clear, however, that the dragon's mouth becomes the
mother's womb.

8.   Networks and connections have broken down. Everything
is collapsing or the dying fall out of everything or into outer space.
Or they are blinded, screened (examined in detail), dissolved.
"It"—such as a visionary event—occurs. Patients need "bridges":
upward, across, into. The rainbow, as a link between heaven and
earth, or the "ladder" (stairway to heaven), may serve as bridges.

9.   The eye beholding them in transition sears, destroys,
shames patients. Some patients wish that the earth would swal-
low them up. However, this negative interpretation of the symbol
of the eye is a deep-seated projection (such as believing the Other
is a dragon. *Draco*, etymologically, comes from the Greek verb
derkesthai [to see clearly]). It means to stand guard with a sharp
serpent's eye. The emotion of being threatened by this gaze is a
projection deeply rooted in human nature. This projection must
be retracted, which occurs, for instance, when the patient sees a
sad, imploring expression in those eyes, perhaps they are filled

with tears. The awe-inspiring eye also forebodes change. The eye in a dream means simply to see and to be seen, to look and to be recognized, to hear and to be heard. There also are also patients who have seen an eye in a triangle without knowing its deep symbolical meaning. Several symbols of eyes have to be considered in this context, such as the eye in an equilateral triangle, which symbolizes Yahweh in the Hebrew tradition, and the "all-seeing eye of God," which represents the Trinity in the Christian tradition, the Masonic symbols, and Islamic symbols, and the like.

10. What a few moments ago was "pitch-black" or "utterly gray" may now escalate into the "epitome of horror" (freezing cold, hellish heat, never-ending moisture, and the like). Sometimes fission occurs: blackness is divided, followed by rupture, movement, evaporation.

11. Seldom do patients feel a curse hanging over them. Changing scenarios in the spiritual struggle are, for instance, the blazing red fire, darkness, or the devil, which all temporarily overwhelm patients. They feel defeated—and yet ultimately they remain unmolested, to emerge unscathed.

What Helps?

In transition itself, patients need caregivers and spiritual guides capable of conveying a sense of reassurance and competence in dealing with the dark, sinister world. Emphatically, such guidance has nothing to do with magic and least of all with exorcistic practices. What helps, in my experience, is if I simply invoke the angels or, if a Christian patient, make the sign of the cross on a patient's forehead or walk a protective circle around his bed, so that the inner child might intuitively understand the clearly symbolic protection. Sometimes it helps if I voice my own sense of the experienced symbolism: "You need a bridge now" or "This chasm is like a devouring dragon's mouth. But you are safe inside and it will open up." Most of all, however, I know from folktales and myths that the dark powers will become thoroughly transformed, symbolically, once the ego capitulates. In transition itself, patients need encouragement and the reassurance that change will happen.

IMPORTANT SYMBOLS IN POST-TRANSITION

Post-transition is characterized by an ineffable peaceful reality pervaded by a noticeably changed atmosphere. All impasses have dissolved, answers are now given. Characteristic symbolic expressions and images include:

1. The sea has become a "wonderful water world," a spherical event, a world of light and color. The forest becomes a "fertile soil" or a "foundation" as such. Out of the desert or from forlornness many patients find their way home and are thus also found. Green pastures, flowering meadows, clouds bearing them aloft.

2. Pipes and tunnels now lie behind the dying. They are surrounded by light, open space, air. Colors become transformed, from gray into silver, from dull into shining metal. The atmosphere can be that of "worshipping at the mount."

3. The dying have completed their crossing. The airplane has landed, and they have found what they were seeking. Now is the time for homecoming or for retreating to a new home or house, an eternal city. A new planet, a garden.

4. The bird has flown off, up and away, or it has landed (out of sight). Patients feel free, free as a bird. The phoenix leaves traces of transformation and fulfillment.

5. Soul cleansing is followed by deference and protection. The dying receive clothes made of the finest linen, a holy writing tablet, and so on. Gold replaces nothingness; gold stands for a deep protection and value—for instance, a gold ring, a crown.

6. The festive dress can symbolize a gift of God or of grace or is no longer important. Patients experience substance, sound, and music beyond the corporeal.

7. Out of the devouring chasm emerges a life-sustaining womb or a great, cradling, motherly whole that lends patients care and protection. Here, in this refuge, the dying are sheltered, safe within, and part of a congenial totality. "An apron as large as the earth that resembles a great womb" (Hebrew *rechem* [womb] can be associated with *rachem* [to have compassion]). The Hebrew word for mercy is related to "womb." The motif of the large hat or of many hats suggests shelter and safekeeping.

8. New networks have arisen, a spiderweb, a mandala, a bright network of communication or lighting. These cables are not man-made. Energy simply exists rather than being "made" artificially. Light, the color yellow, a silver gloss, spirit (e.g., "And the city had no need of the sun, neither of the moon, to shine in it, for the glory of God did lighten it" [Rev. 21:23]). The rainbow as a symbol of peace that unites all colors.

9. The eye epitomizes a Thou and "loves me." We experience a sense of community, of belonging. The rainbow as a symbol of confederation.

10. Dissolution into light, into the colors yellow, gold, blue, azure, green, and violet. Every color is without boundaries.

11. Divisions have been overcome. The curse is banned, the devil has dissolved, is dead, or has vanished. Angels have defeated darkness.

What we have yearned for now occurs: the feast, the celebration, the wedding, splendor, heavenly music. The dying are invited, a table is prepared for them (Ps. 23:5). There is an atmosphere of abundance, peace, connectedness.

6

THE SITES OF TRANSITION

Fear, Struggle, Acceptance,
Family Processes, Maturation

W HAT HINDERS and what facilitates the dying process? In the discussions with the two palliative care
physicians Florian Strasser and Daniel Bueche
during our project "Dying Is a Transition" (Renz, Schuett Mao,
Bueche, Cerny, and Strasser 2013) five factors or dimensions of
transition emerged: fear, struggle, denial and acceptance, family
processes, and maturation.

FEAR

Primordial fear is a threshold-specific emotion, an essential aspect
of transition, a challenge that we have to take on (chapter 3).
The dying need to pass through this barrier. Gripped by threshold
fear, they can only capitulate. Threshold fear can be more or less
pronounced. Indication-oriented palliative care is aligned with
patients' symptoms and is also focused on the inner process of
dying. It not only considers their verbal hints but also tries to understand their nonverbal signals, and responds with adequate medical, and therapeutic-spiritual support. Such indication-oriented

care is more than needs-based, more than purely symptom-based. Crucially, it also facilitates transition. Today, however, most people are unaware of transition and threshold fear. This fear has hitherto been neglected in public discussions about good dying.

By contrast, other fears are often expressed. Confronted with a terminal illness or with a relative disfigured by illness, many people voice their conscious fears (e.g., of helplessness and pain) and rebel against what is commonly seen as an undignified existence. Some express fear of the uncertainty in death and of what comes afterward. The findings of "Dying Is a Transition" (N = 80/600) (appendix, table) are interesting in this respect: whereas only a small number of patients (14%/10%) expressed or indicated a fear of uncertainty, a significantly greater number (35%/50%) said that they were afraid of powerlessness, pain, and symptoms. But this was not all: a similar number of patients (38%/44%) were overcome by transitional, primordial fear (chapter 3), including many patients who had previously expressed no fear of death. Fear, then, seems to be unforeseeable. For the remaining patients, we have no clear hints about their fear; perhaps they felt fear, perhaps not. We lack any significant signals of their experience. Interpreting these results suggests that neither uncertainty (about the afterlife) nor the fact of dying (the end of life) seems to be the main problem for patients, but their fear of symptoms, and the described threshold experience (chapter 3), which seems to overwhelm them unexpectedly. Not dying is taboo, but suffering is. Patients, relatives, and the public need authoritative and reliable information about how palliative medicine contributes to alleviating suffering and about the emotional and spiritual opening (Kuhl 2002) that might happen inwardly during the dying process. Both the fundamentally other state of consciousness and being, and in consequence the three states of transition (pre-transition, transition itself, post-transition), need to be better understood and integrated into care concepts and research. Patients and relatives find explanations of these states and the comparison to near-death experiences very helpful. Many are grateful to learn that fear and pain have an end, because hardly any pain sensitivity and sense of powerlessness exist beyond ego-based perception. Whereas a disfigured body looks unsightly, within the soul and the spirit something utterly different or even magnificent may be occurring at the same time. This much we know from many near-death experiences, which happen when the body is on the verge of extinction (Lommel 2010). I observe similar phenomena in deathbed experiences week after week (see also Fenwick and Brayne 2011).

Every time before he was admitted to hospital, Toni Tanner, a middle-aged man, suffered the same trauma: he trembled, vomited, had difficulty breathing, and was panic-stricken with fear. These were exactly the same experiences that his father had exhibited when he lay on his deathbed and could not die. He (the father) had looked dreadful, his eyes filled with suffering; in the end he lay silently, eyes closed, emaciated, and yet death would still not come. Ever since witnessing his father dying, Toni Tanner knew that he wanted never to suffer in the same way. When I mentioned the states of consciousness and being, (pre-transition versus the post-transitional experience beyond the ego), he listened fascinated, and remarked: "Are you saying that my father suffered less than those who watched him die?" He wanted to reflect on this. Soon afterward, Toni Tanner's traumatic stress ceased.

Linda Lütholf, an elderly woman, whose extreme fear of her cancer spreading had once bordered on paranoia and who had needed psychiatric treatment, became almost perfectly serene in going toward her death. She knew instinctively how close to death she was. She did, however, suffer several bouts of fear on her deathbed: she gazed into the distance, her face writhed, her metastasis-ridden leg grew restless, she was racked with pain. Yet these symptoms soon disappeared, and she enjoyed her husband's visits and my harp-playing. She was also soothed when we reminded her of her own guardian angel and, as she was a Roman Catholic, of the statue of the Virgin Mary standing in the Chapel of Mercy at Einsiedeln, the famous pilgrimage site. Tears rolled down her cheeks, then she smiled at me and said my name. Mostly, she seemed far removed from the here and now, her eyebrows raised in astonishment. She grew increasingly fond of silence. She died one night peacefully and alone, presumably without fear.

Such fears are suffered by the child within us. But it is enough to remind that child of a greater refuge, which may be conveyed through silent presence, music, or signs and rituals representing protection (on the structure of fear, see Renz 2008a: pt. 1, chap. 6).

STRUGGLE

The struggle with death is similar to and yet different from the fear of death. Some patients struggling with death come up against their individual structures of desire and power (Renz 2008a). Then they have difficulties in letting themselves go. Others find themselves amid a spiritual struggle between angels and evil forces, where higher powers are grappling with each other.

A knowledge of the book of Daniel, or of the images in the book of Revelation of John, helps some spiritual caregivers to better grasp the spiritual distress of the dying. The book of Revelation offers consolation: its lengthy descriptions of horror bear witness to the fact that there is triumph or victory in transition. As mentioned in the introduction (see note 3), many images in scriptures are not primarily a matter of belief and faith but their metaphors and successions of symbols are an expression of our dream consciousness (see figure A.3). Richard Rohr (2011) talks about the deeper meaning of myth and folktales which belong to a so-called deep time (reaching beyond our own time and culture). Exactly dying patients teach us this lesson. A notable example is the motif of spiritual struggle and victory, which is experienced by agnostics as well. Regardless of whether they represent a last truth or not, these metaphors influence patients, and they can be resolved by understanding their inherent logic (Turner 1969; van Gennep 1909). Victory, for example, is a word of command and denotes a power structure. Yet such victory in dying, is not a victory within the ego but instead a triumph amid capitulation and beyond. Spiritual care and rituals in such situations have to be based on understanding this dynamic. For instance, the Archangel Michael (leader of the guard who stood with the sons of Israel [Dan. 12:1]) or the great Light in many near-death experiences, or the "king of kings, and lord of lords" (Rev. 19:16), can stand for bringing resolution and redemption. Caregivers can call these angels and powers, as well as pray, give a blessing, or perform any other ritual of consolation. In many shamanistic healing rituals, music is the means of mediation between heaven and earth.

One elderly patient reported that she had to surrender. At this moment, she felt part of a triumph but that the victory did not belong to her. That is precisely how such struggles end: victory seems to emerge as if we are both driven and drawn by a final goal; heading for disaster thus turns into an invitation to partake of the whole.

———

As the dying teach us, there seems to be an inner law: As soon as the ego surrenders, it partakes of such victory. Thus in our essence, our innermost being, we are once again united with the totality of our creator, creation, and creatureliness in a new way. The dying experience this reunion and call it, for example, "fate brought to a good, well-rounded conclusion," "the perceived deeper meaning lying behind the incomprehensible," "the inner greatness of the suffering endured." Such connectedness is more than mere consolation. It is the highest accolade possible. It is victory. My study (N = 80/600) revealed that the phenomenon of struggle, so difficult to grasp, was experienced by 30% of patients (appendix, table). Some patients referred explicitly to this elusive phenomenon, whereas others "fought the battle" restlessly, their agitation indicating more than fear.

The apocalyptic struggle with death, then, is neither only a theological construct nor simply a figment of the imagination among naive believers but is instead an actual experience among the dying. As a reality, such struggles occur regardless of faith or religious affiliation, and they are experienced not just by those who are in a final rebellion against death. Similar to fear, this struggle also besets those dying who, owing to their strength of personality, experience an extraordinary awakening of consciousness and an initiation into the depths of being. This kind of death struggle is at the same time a profound initiation and final vocation, which occurs in any religion or faith. One example from the Hebrew tradition is Isaiah 6:1–13 ("In the year that King Uzziah died . . .").

Leaders of other religions and traditions may wish to add their own examples of vocation and thereby focus on inherent rules and workings. Fear or struggle? Critical minds may find it somewhat far-fetched to finely discriminate between fear and struggle in these episodes. Whereas fear is primarily an emotional problem, struggle is a spiritual one. Exactly this distinction shows that there seem to be two levels of experience: the emotional and the spiritual. Keeping this in mind is important for end-of-life caregivers even if patients always talk about fear, and even if the symptoms are similar to fear (they tremble, cry out, and suffer acute attacks of pain). Nevertheless, behind all that often stands more than fear.

How, then, can we distinguish struggle from fear? Fear—whose opposite emotion is trust—can often be resolved and calmed down by words of protection and consolation. In contrast, patients amid struggle are sometimes restless, prone to tossing and turning, and find no peace. Their inner oscillation between refusal and acceptance manifests itself bodily. Struggle is called for at the crossroads of a spiritual path; its opposite is inner peace. Struggle has to be struggled through and endured. What matters quite literally in the death struggle is the "discerning of spirits," "discernment between Light and Darkness," or "motions of the soul" (Ignatius Loyola). Observing patients in their final struggle has taught me that such discernment and distinction actually take place. Even though the fear of death is socially accepted, it falls far short of capturing the dynamics involved: fear is an emotion that we are afraid of and evade, but struggle is an event that sends shivers down our spine. Whereas fear involves our inner child, struggle exposes patients to feeling threatened by energetic realities (such as colossal forces, irrational powers and forces, the struggle between Light and Darkness). Apropos of these realities, I earlier referred to some sequences of metaphors (chapter 5).

Caregivers can help by addressing the spiritual dimension and by encouraging patients to fight on until it is time to give up or until the coming of the angels. When patients hesitate, I often say: "Don't stop, keep going." Or I explain, "You have the choice between lying there abjectly or accepting and being defeated." Experience teaches me that "it" (never knowing what exactly) opens precisely when we surrender. I often use the image of jumping: "All you can do now is jump from a diving board into the unknown, into water or darkness. But I know from experience that if you do so, there will be softness and light." If patients struggle for hours, I am sometimes called on to insist, "Go on, push, jump, give it a try. . . . It will be beautiful."

———

Priska Petermann, a woman about forty-five years old, an agnostic, was unable to die or take leave of her husband and daughter, let alone her lust and greed for life. She clutched at everything, greedily sucking it, even though her doctors attested that her craving thirst was not a medical issue, as is sometimes the case. Her fear was enormous. "Doesn't anyone understand me?" she cried into the empty room. A few days later, she seemed to be "on the other side," somnolent but still responsive. Now, she muttered, she would die, she could see the gate, it was yellow. But minutes later, her ego and its greed had taken hold of her again. She was shaking. "Not die," she exclaimed, and then she wanted to "die right now." Her hands reached out to mine and gripped them firmly as if she were frightened. "Are you falling into yourself?" I asked. "Oh yes!" she replied. I recounted an episode from the folktale about Mother Hulda (chapter 2, note 1). Did she know the tale? "Ahh," she sighed. I said that there, too, someone falls into a well, that Gold Mary jumps into the well, terrified, but on reaching the bottom she finds a meadow covered in a thousand flowers, the oven filled with baked

bread, and ripe apples hanging from the tree. Most of all, however, down there lives good Mother Hulda. There was no fear there,
and the soul could "have" whatever it needed. Priska Petermann
listened and then beamed, before drifting off for several minutes.
On coming back, she confirmed, "Mother . . . Meadow. Enough.
Mmmh." She surfaced into the present and subsided again several times, each time helped by the tale—the image of the meadow
("green"), the aspect of replenishment ("mmmh"), the good Great
Mother ("Mama, Hulda"). Beside her bed, her husband stood
astounded by such satisfaction and was reassured, at least for the
time being.

When I was called to Priska Petermann the next day and heard
that she was afraid, I recognized struggle. Her body was tossing
and turning. "Not . . . ," she exclaimed, affirming that she did not
want to die. How could anyone who knew of the little children
whom she would leave behind not understand her plight? But
this did not seem to be her major concern. When I mentioned her
children, she did not respond. Nothing now reached the screaming
woman. At loose ends, I finally dared to ask her if she was angry at
God. "Yesss." She tossed and turned, and looked up at me, aghast.
Was it terrible where she was? "Ahh!" I felt my way forward, asking further questions, until I realized that Priska Petermann
was engulfed in devouring darkness that must have seemed evil.
Regardless of whether she understood me or not, I told her that
it was normal for her to feel this way, adding that it was a matter of entering the darkness. Gold Mary, I reminded her, had also
jumped into the dark well. I added that suddenly everything would
be light, and she would be cared for, maybe by angels. Saying this,
I invoked the angels, and then told the agnostic and intellectual
Priska Petermann about the Archangel Michael, who is depicted
as a chief prince (Dan. 10:13) and who will appear in the last days

and fight the dragon (Rev. 12:7). Here, Priska Petermann pricked up her ears. Her gaze moved as if to encircle the contours of something she had seen with her mind's eye, and then her eyes closed again. After slowly breathing in and out, her body calmed and her muscle tone was soft within a few minutes, and a kind of wise smile crossed her face. She uttered one last word: "Greeeen." Had Priska Petermann—by letting herself fall—found Mother Hulda's meadow, the life force and the "green force" (Riedel 1989:37)? Had she been initiated into the mystery of dying and renewal? She lay there for another two days before dying peacefully.

———

———

The case of Paula Panhofer, a young mother and a once-elegant woman now facing death, was similar yet somewhat different. The concern for her small boys would not let go of this frail, terminally ill woman. To begin with, she did not want to die. Weeks later she could not die, even though rationally she would have been ready to do so. Again and again, acute attacks of restlessness and pain made it difficult for her to let go. Her young children were reluctant to come to her bedside, which almost seemed to hurt her. But why? Was this perhaps a key to her lingering, to what was keeping her from dying? Good foster parents had been found, her husband reassured her, but his words did not seem to reach the absent-minded, apathetic woman. Eventually, I said to her: "Perhaps you need to hear, quite rightly, that you have been a good mother, that your efforts have not been in vain, and that there will be no undoing by death. Your motherly love will live on in your boys and in your husband." Introducing the notion of God as the Whole, I added: "God will not ignore your mothering. You were, more than anything else, a mother. That was your life's work."

Her breathing intensified, followed by a gentle sound when she exhaled. She lay there for two more days, completely serene, and then she crossed over.

———

FROM REBELLION TO ACCEPTANCE

Dying also involves falling into an all-encompassing "yes." This "yes" is a basic or indeed final condition, which embraces or underlies all individual negations and affirmations. Karl Rahner (1982:175–176) speaks of a fundamental decision that remains anonymous, or of a fundamental act of uttermost freedom (2004:142–151). Whereas that "yes" needs to be searched for and found, mercy comes into play when the dying find their way from taking action themselves to allowing things to happen.

"Still" and "yet": these two small words, which sometimes cross the lips of terminally ill patients, afford us a sense of the threshold situation. "I am still here," "It isn't time for me yet," "No, no, not yet," "Still another week, another week," is what patients tell us when they are not yet ready to die. While looking toward the threshold, the ego perceives the impending death and change, comparable to a "gathering storm" but still resists the approaching danger, being strong enough to do so. Everything is still home and dry. Here, in the "still" or "not yet," the ego bides its time. The dying look back, then again forward to the threshold, hesitate, and allow themselves to be lured by the possibilities of prolonging life and of indulging ego-centered pleasures (a good meal, take a ride in a sports car, spending time with one's partner). Some dying people allow themselves to be detained to the point of weariness: they vomit their food, the ride is painful and vertigo-inducing, the time spent with one's partner proves to be dreary. This goes on until the

ego's time has definitely "run out" and patients may ask, "I wonder what is coming." When the ego has ceased asking the same
questions about destiny and meaning, ceased asking or wanting or
thinking . . . indeed, ceased feeling its usual needs, when the desir-
ing, thinking, self-caring ego has let itself fall, it thereby enters
transition (about falling and transformation in midlife and old
age, see Rohr 2011). There it is found, mysteriously, by that "yes," by
that acceptance we can never deliberately choose but is given to us
by life. The "yes" need not even be uttered. Instead it can simply be
lived or "breathed" imperceptibly.

The process of acceptance described by Elisabeth Kübler-
Ross (1974; denial, anger, bargaining, depression, acceptance; see
chapter 2) may become relevant time and again—after receiving a
diagnosis, after every stroke of fate, and eventually before accepting death. Each time it is experienced more consciously. Enduring this process time and again during illness helps the dying
person as a familiar energy pathway. Repeatedly thrust back and
forth, we are challenged to let go in order to "bring home" life and
suffering (Nouwen 1998:94). Finding our way into lived acceptance can be understood as a profound becoming one with ourselves and with all being. From an existential perspective, death
acceptance may happen when a person has moved from self-
actualization to "self-transcendence, as a movement beyond oneself" (Tomer, Eliason, and Wong 2008:443; see also Wong 2008).

On its deepest level, acceptance is a spiritual agreement, and a
vibrational, musical harmony (chapter 4). It is a state of "being in
harmony" and at peace, of understanding and being understood.
As a fundamentally inner act, this "yes" is differently grounded,
more corporeal than the spoken word. It encompasses, once
again, all that has been. It means saying "yes" to myself and my
existence, to life in my body, its unsightliness and illnesses. It is

a "yes" to my formative influences, my fear, my childhood; a "yes" to those people and institutions who have hurt me; a "yes" to our culture and its bonds; and a "yes" even to my guilt and limitations. Ultimately, this immensely difficult acceptance is a "yes" to creation, creator, and creature, to death, and also to suffering. Not because suffering is heroic, but because it is real. This existential "yes" is not a fatalism that leaves one without desire or incapable of change. Nor does it involve removal from reality or asceticism. Instead, this "yes" liberates, in life as in dying, to experience grace and power, sensuousness, and gratitude. It frees, in life and in dying, from waiting and entrapment, from the increasingly longer shadow of the past into the future and beyond.

In this "yes," we recognize not only humility and *kenosis* (emptying) but also courage and personality. We cannot ask this of ourselves too rashly. Attaining this "yes" occurs not without tears, sometimes not without struggles, nor once and for all. Nevertheless, as soon as one is capable of wanting this affirmation, it then amounts to a spiritual victory in life as in dying. Dorothee Sölle (pers. comm., November 2001) has formulated this victory as follows: "'Wanting' is a fundamental spiritual term." Our decision to "want" to reach this destination, sometime and somehow, opens ourselves up to change. Patients often tell me that they—affirmatively—find their way "home." The dying who have thus found their way home bear witness to a great change in their condition and perception. Pain, tension, and other bodily symptoms are now past. What they intuit as a subject and as an opposed object also changes frequently. The path to this state can be plain and undramatic. It often occurs quietly, perhaps secretly.

Anna Abel, who was about sixty years old, was restless. I tried to understand what was preoccupying her and at some point asked her, "Isn't it quite understandable that we cannot simply say 'yes'?" She looked straight at me, almost frightened. Had I "hurt" her feelings? She continued to look straight at me. Gently, I suggested that she did not need to say "yes" to please me, or her husband, or her parents, or indeed God. But experience had taught me, I added, that saying "yes" made us feel better. Did she want to try, perhaps secretly, while breathing out? Anna Abel still held my gaze as if my suggestion made sense. Perhaps she did try, she became somnolent until she passed away quietly.

————

Our study (see appendix, table) revealed that the process of acceptance was crucial (69%/90%). Among the remaining patients such a process could not be ruled out, but it was not plainly evident. Where the process was apparent, it was differently nuanced. A first subgroup underwent the typical process from rebellion to acceptance (30%/45%), while a second subgroup expressed prolonged or total denial (24%/33%), and also seemed to suffer from pain and tension. Only a minority (15%/12%) were just ready to die; presumably, they had undergone their process of acceptance earlier.

We can practice the all-encompassing "yes" already during our lifetime. When I give lectures on dying, I am repeatedly asked whether we cannot tackle the difficult tasks that present themselves in dying before our time comes. We can but at the same time we cannot, I reply. We can practice mindfulness, in the truest sense of the word—that is, live consciously, sensuously, and keep our hearts and minds open to everyday joy and to hidden meaningfulness even in suffering. We can attune ourselves to the great "yes." Many psalms do so by praising God, or the Creator, or the Numinous. From praise and the act of acceptance emerges the energy pathway that in effect will eventually help us in the dying process. I have observed time and again that people whose religious faith means trust and affirmation are borne along by their faith in the process of dying. Nonetheless, if patients do adhere to a doctrinal faith, then they are challenged to let go of dogma first. Every fixation has to be let go before dying: the fixation on one's mother or dog, for instance, or a fixed notion of God.

To what extent, however, can we not prepare for dying? Dying is an unpredictable and individual act of being overwhelmed and surprised. Dying remains a mystery. Even after providing end-of-life care for more than fifteen years, I must remain open to just how much fear and how much "initiation" will be asked of me when my time comes. "Fear not," say the angels frequently in the Bible and maybe also in the scriptures of other religions and ethnic groups. The angel symbolizes the boundary state itself, as a bridge across and as a messenger between two worlds. By announcing to us, "Fear not," the angel tells us indirectly that at this place and threshold fear or better awe is appropriate. Such a word does indeed offer consolation.

FAMILY PROCESSES, FAREWELLS, RECONCILIATION

Dying is also a farewell. Because it ends life, it is never harmless but conclusive and unique. Already the passage toward death reveals an increasing intensity not just within the dying but also in family members. At some point, it is as if everything within the dying were focused on the invisible transition. This explains why initially (in pre-transition) many dying persons, compelled by the proximity of death, make farewell arrangements, draw up a last will, yearn for reconciliation, and expect family processes to occur as never before. They wish to clarify the "record" and to die "released." On the other hand, these transitional events help to explain why at some point relatives become amazingly irrelevant (in transition itself, which can be compared with birth and labor pains, and even more so in post-transition): spending time together is over, and our being together is transformed.

One exception is an acute family problem, such as a patient's reluctance to leave a problem child all on its own, or worrying about a seriously ill or traumatized child, or suffering under an unresolved family dispute. Sometimes worrying may prevent patients from dying. Certain family concerns can be the background to bodily pain (total pain), restlessness, resistance, struggle, and despair.

Our study (see appendix, table) revealed that family processes were important in the majority of cases (82%/78%); we found no unequivocal signals among the other respondents. For 51%/52% of these, relatives were important in pre-transition but no longer near death; and the other 31%/26% suffered from unresolved family problems, which hindered the process of dying. The dying then needed support for themselves and their relatives. Whenever problems were resolved, the dying could continue in the process from pre-transition or transition itself to post-transition.

––––––

Boris Bader, a sixty-year-old patient, had been unresponsive for two days. He was groaning, breath by breath. No medication, not even sedation, was able to calm him. This seriously affected the nursing staff. Why this agony? The Bader family had continually refused therapeutic assistance, but now they sought my help. Everything had always been in order in their Roman Catholic family, they told me. Somewhat anxiously, Boris Bader's children remarked that they had distanced themselves from home. Their mother had died two years earlier. The atmosphere was tense, and I found out precious little about the personality of their dying father. What had mattered to him during his lifetime? Then, an old girlfriend came to visit him, and the groaning sound in his breathing intensified. Could she tell me more about Boris Bader? Much was kept silent in this family, she told me. "Hhhhh," he responded. What actually was kept silent? Who remained silent? She had never had a sexual relationship with Boris Bader, his friend added, but they had been fond of each other. His wife had erected a wall of stone around herself and remained silent for days when she found out about her husband and his friend. In fact, Boris Bader and his wife had never talked about the matter, or anything else really important in life. Now, he continued to groan, and I had a strange feeling that he was listening. I asked him if he had never defended himself or screamed? "Heeeh!" he cried out from his depths, the sound rolling on and on. This was probably the scream that had never come out. Boris Bader could not die as a petrified man, but letting out that cry helped him to let go of himself. I suggested that his dead wife might understand his outcry wherever/whoever she was now. His rolling outcry slowly subsided. Did he understand, and was he understood?

Lorenz Lehner, a father of several children, was also unable to die. He lay on his deathbed for three weeks, motionless and comatose. "What was the problem?" his wife asked me. Everything had been taken care of. His children had been to visit, and he had reacted to each of them. I asked his wife about her husband's life. What kind of a person had he been? Full of life, shy, hardworking—and he had never forgotten his son from his first marriage. But this

son was now in a mental hospital. And his wife had not wanted
him to visit his father. I said that I could understand that such
an encounter must be difficult for her, but that probably it was
important for her husband, as a father, at least to hear about
this child. Could she perhaps find out how this son was doing?
Reluctant but nonetheless moved by the seriousness of the situation, she accepted my suggestion. The next day she returned and
said, "I don't know where Fabian is. I couldn't find out anything."
I believed her. But what could be done? I asked, "Does your husband believe in God?" "Not directly, but he did somehow. He
liked sitting in an empty church." We went to her husband's room.
His wife remained mute and motionless, so I encouraged her,
"Say your name and that you are here." I also introduced myself.
Lorenz Lehner did not react. I addressed him directly: "All your
children have been to visit, except Fabian . . ." I could not fin-
ish the sentence because his groaning interrupted me. His wife,
startled, said, "But he can hear!" "Of course, he can. He is present, he is waiting," I insisted. Turning again to the patient, I said,
"Mr. Lehner, God is so great that Fabian also has his place, wher-
ever he may be now. And Fabian had a father who never forgot
him. This does not escape the eyes of God." Thereafter followed
more groaning, then deep breathing, and a few hours later this
father was able to die.

MATURATION

For some dying persons, who find themselves in pre-transition
and looking ahead toward their demise, it is important to conduct
a life review, as if there existed an inner urge toward an invisible goal. For precisely now, at last, fragments of personality must

be united; what has eluded understanding now asks to be understood. The accidental searches for meaning; what has fallen by the wayside now yearns to be embraced and made part of life, and the unexpressed now calls for expression. That is why many dying are faced with the need for maturation and integration, and why they accept this challenge. But biography work at the deathbed (in contrast to the last weeks and months, see Chochinov et al. 2005; Kuhl 2002) remains, and needs to remain, imperfect and fragmentary. Therapeutic ambition is out of place there.

"Everything wants a place in my prayers," the elderly Michael Meier told me tearfully: the war years, his first love, his marriage and his wife, their childlessness, the never-ending, toilsome work on construction sites. He had written down everything for his funeral. "And what will happen to all my stamps?" he asked me sadly. Did I not know of anyone, perhaps a boy, to whom he could give his collection? What was to become of his life's work, its joy and suffering? We found a young heir for the collection; the dying man could then pass on his stamps and work, praying, "Father, into thy hands I commend my stamps, my love, my spirit." I was reminded of the last words of Jesus on the cross (Luke 23:46). Michael Meier's inner process of transition could now proceed as he said: "through—a long hollow tube—across."

Do we need concepts such as final maturation on the deathbed, coming to full growth or development, post-maturing? Do such words have any meaning for us? Can the dying not just die as they are? Of course they can, and we must never confront the dying with such questions. But sometimes maturation happens, and when it does we need to honor it. And sometimes maturation is needed for the ongoing process, then we can try to initiate it. Maturation on the deathbed is both "post-maturation" (coming to full maturity at the end of life) and a final maturing into the quest for meaning, order, and integration. Sometimes this is experienced as freeing oneself, sometimes as a healing from the wounds of life, work, relationships, and even violence and trauma. Unfortunately, it is precisely at this stage, when illness leaves patients utterly helpless, that traumatic experiences of powerlessness long past are reactivated. "When my mother died . . . ," "During the war, when I was covered in debris . . ." Where there is language, traumas remain present in the semiconscious and are accessible to therapy. When language has ceased, only symptoms are left—cramped posture, expressions of fright, pervasive defense reactions. Thus a well-trained psychotherapeutic eye, and an atmosphere, which allows healing and to heal, are most important in attending to the dying.

Maria Mathis, in her mid-fifties, lay half-bent on her bed, staring into the corner. Her rosary lay next to her, untouched. The telephone rang; she flinched. Her position had remained unchanged for two days. No sooner had the nurses changed her position than she would reassume and go on staring into the corner. What, I wondered, could this strange posture mean? I was clueless. She showed no reaction. Eventually, I adopted the same position, as best I could, and also stared into the corner. "What?" she interrupted the leaden silence. I repeated, while amplifying her question, "What is there? Who is there?" She was unable to answer my questions. Silently her trauma and fright confronted me inwardly. Based on my experience with other traumatized patients, I tried to feel my way toward whatever spook or spirit was deranging her. Was it some evil person, man or woman, an image of an evil animal, or a ghost? Despite these difficult events, which she had probably experienced in the past, her feelings were quite normal, I reassured her. "Hhh, hhh," she uttered, in fits and starts. Did she feel somewhat understood? I took her rosary, made the sign of the cross, first in the air, then on her forehead, then in the corner. Then I said the following words: "God is stronger than all evil, God is protecting you." "Hhh, hhh." Did she want me to make more signs of the cross? "Hhh!" I made the sign on her forehead and hand. Did she want me to do this on other parts of her body? "Yes." Maria Mathis held toward me one part of her body after another: her arm, leg, back, behind. She relaxed. I called the priest and asked him to perform the last rites, which—although she had been anointed on several occasions previously—now touched her deeply, as if for the first time. "Hhh." Maria Mathis died peacefully the next day.

———

For other patients, maturation means enduring transformation and allowing oneself to be overcome by sadness. They weep, and in weeping they silently come to terms with matters, until the tears dry up, the voice softens, and consolation and fatigue begin. The dying also have spiritual needs. For Richard Rohr (2011), the second half of life generally means maturation and a spiritual journey. In approaching death, this dynamic growth intensifies: the soul yearns to become whole, and to find meaning and hope beyond the ego's range. Our follow-up study (see appendix, table) found that 62% of the patients surveyed experienced and expressed themes of maturation (we had not yet introduced this umbrella term in our pilot study; again, the dark number of unreported maturation processes is high). Nearly half of our respondents in both studies reflected on their life (46%/49%). Maturation occurred whenever patients accepted their life—and the here and now; the dying process then continued. Some patients (19%/20%, partly the same patients who reflected on their lives) had to cope with trauma and needed support, some patients (31%/30%, again partly the same patients who reflected on their lives) experienced individuation and found meaning.

A young mother, who had given so much to her disabled, only child, asked herself, "What will happen to my child?" However, the following questions seemed even more important: What would become of the love that she had given her child? Who saw, who appreciated this love? Then we spoke about religion. Religion meant precious little to her generation, she asserted, and asked me, "What does the kingdom of Jesus Christ mean? Why was Moses in the rush basket? Why are just the poor blessed?" She said she failed to understand. It became important for her to imagine God as all-encompassing Whole, which her love could fall neither through nor out of. She rediscovered several images of the Bible, for example, the Last Judgment as "reverence from within": "It has been seen," she summed up matters briefly and, after she had taken that step, fatigue and somnolence prevailed.

THE LIMITS OF END-OF-LIFE CARE

Time and again, we fail to get through to the dying. Their symbolic gestures elude us, their tension fails to dissolve. Besides, there are also those patients who refuse any form of help or who reject us as caregivers anyhow, regardless of their worldview. Time and again, there are patients who hardly allow themselves to be touched by nursing staff and cannot bear visits, least of all from psychologists or pastors. Even medical assistance or medication sometimes falls short. What to do?

Put differently, what happens to the dying who, as we see it, die amid fighting? The face is contorted, or a scream seems to stifle the sufferer to death. Have we failed in such cases? Or even worse, are these persons denied inner happiness and resolution?

Fortunately, death remains a definitive boundary, beyond which we can neither see nor judge. My inability to help a dying person when "accompanying" him on his last path says nothing conclusive about his essence and experience, but merely about my limitations. What, for instance, does *time* mean? When does timelessness begin? Where does the unbearable boundlessness cease and wonderful eternity begin? What does *space* mean exactly? Where does it begin, and where does it end? How do we experience space beyond our bodily awareness? When exactly do the dying feel they are inside their body, and when not? What is their sense of pain? And where does their fear subside? In analogy to out-of-body experiences I would like to introduce the term "out-of-fear experience." Concerning the beginning and ending of our sense of time, space, body, fear, pain, and symptoms, I refer again to the account of the two rock-climbing mountaineers (chapter 2).

Another mountaineer who was admitted to our hospital lay in a coma after a fall. He described this event as an experience of pure color: "There were no longer individual objects like an alpenstock, a stone, my body, or the mountain lake, but instead colors, as if they were detached from their forms: everything was pure blue, and at the same time there was pure yellow." Later, the man associated the color blue with the sky, and yellow with the sun and the stars. These colors had surrounded him, indeed flooded him, and they seemed to dance. Then everything turned green, at which point he instantaneously gained a sense of his body and corporeality. He had returned to life. However dreadful he had looked, his experience—he told me—was highly spiritual.

Similarly, we do not exactly know what goes on inside disfigured patients nor inside those whom we fail to reach. We do well to acknowledge the blank in our perceptions and, after all, we are also allowed to be human beings with limits.

7

DYING WITH DIGNITY

Indication-Oriented End-of-Life Care

OVERVIEW

Dying is more than physical extinction. More occurs in dying than meets the eye. This book has claimed that human perception changes fundamentally in the process of dying: from ego-based perception, and from ego-centered experience, to a state of being beyond the ego, as well as beyond fear and pain. I have discussed the categorical differences between these two modes of perception and experience, as far as this is at all possible from our limited human perspective.

Between these two modes of being lies a threshold in consciousness, mythologically speaking a flaming sword, a baptism of fire, a crossing through water. Dying, I have argued, is characterized predominantly by a threshold experience.

Contrary to Elisabeth Kübler-Ross (1974), whose five-stage model of the dying process focuses on our ability to accept a stroke of fate, this book has described three phenomenologically distinct stages of dying, all of which concern the fundamental experience of a threshold: pre-transition (before the threshold and with the end in view), transition itself (passage across this threshold), and post-transition (after this threshold yet still in this world). Thereby ego-centered perception is transformed. These three stages have been discussed in detail, including the associated mental states and emotions of dying persons. I have explored the difficulties, beauties, and especially the experiences of dignity lived through by the dying, as well as their concrete statements about such experiences.

This book has revealed that the threshold to death constitutes, quite naturally, an inner obstacle. Not always, but often. Some dying persons experience this obstacle more consciously and more powerfully than others. The obstacle implies more than visible aspects such as making a will, family processes, and symptom control. What I have referred to as primordial fear makes intelligible what can be so difficult in dying and in crossing this threshold: the invisible experience of a resonating, numinous Other and of utter forlornness. I have also discussed the "language" in which the dying live and are reachable in their distinct hearing sensitivity, and in their symbolic world. Then, I have listed sequences of frequent symbols (chapter 5) and discussed various factors of this transformation, including the sites where such change takes place: fear, struggle, the question of acceptance, the significance of family processes in moving toward death, and maturation (life review, trauma healing, finding meaning) (chapter 6). What I have referred to as primordial care and for the public discussion about good dying and good death. In this context I want to shed light on some difficulties of leaving, and of leaving behind "this world" and its specific laws and workings.

LEAVE-TAKING FROM THIS WORLD
AND ITS PLEASURES

In dying, the ego stands reflexively in its own way. This claim is based on the interpretation of the words and signals uttered by patients. Leave-taking means more than just bidding farewell to close relatives, our home, our beloved dog, or the nursing staff we have grown fond of. More fundamentally, this concerns taking leave from "this world and its pleasures." The human ego (at least as shaped by the Abrahamic religions and Western culture, as well as the ego of subsequent generations of migrants) struggles to detach itself from worldly pleasures, urges, and achievements. Western human nature has evidently grounded itself so radically in the ego world—mythologically, on this side of Eden—that it knows nothing else (see figure A.3, nothing of the shaded area and the area beneath). Precisely this makes the threshold of transition so total. It explains why many dying persons shrink back and return to the present, to remain among us, to be "I" again; not happily, but biding their time instead. Although they fail to understand what is happening to them, still they cannot die. Richard Rohr (2011:65–72) talks about letting the "Life-God-Grace-Mystery" transform the ego. In dying, our formative experiences and even our human condition, both of which I have spoken of elsewhere (Renz 2008a, 2009), are transformed. Reflexively, something inside us "defies" or "desires," indeed wants to "have," even before we consciously realize it and even when we die.

Given these insights, caution is warranted when considering the needs of the dying, and when developing only a needs-based care approach. What is a real need and what, by contrast, is only a triggered reflex? If I tickle a person, she will laugh, even though she may not feel like laughing. The needs and narcissisms of the dying should no longer be awakened, as happened with a patient in his mid-thirties: He had actually made the transitional process twice, spoke of a tunnel and luminous figures, and asked me every day why he could not die. Then two nurses and the patient teased one another. Already before this mischief, and even more so afterward, he was sexually stimulated and craved some "fun." The game had "turned him on," and the unsuspecting nurses were pleased. That evening, he felt "hungover," as if after a party. He was very bad-tempered and sad. The world of the ego "had him in its clutches again" for several days—not in a fit and mentally healthy state, however, but in a pitiful, pain-ridden condition. Is such a prolongation of life desirable?

In an interview one young woman gave shortly before dying, she spontaneously expressed her final wish: to go out for a drive in a sports car. Her wish was granted. On her return, she repeated five times how "great" it had been, but in a toneless voice, and then proceeded to vomit incessantly for days. Had the drive been too much? The care team discussed the question, but the patient refused to consider the issue. Were we asking the wrong question? One morning, after the tension had eased, I asked her: "The drive was cool, wasn't it, but perhaps still a mistake? Did you want an intense experience, though not in this world but in the other world?" She almost cried out: "Yes, exactly." Her comment was followed by digestive noises, which indicated a releasing of tension. The young woman now took leave of her ego-centered reflexes in the knowledge of attaining another kind of desire. Hour after hour, minute after minute, her body became quieter. She fell asleep, reliving transition in the form of bodily restlessness but safely on her way to her final hours of peace and somnolence. She died much sooner than her doctors had predicted.

A dying hospice patient was still able to paint. She painted and painted, and the colors brought her truly back into life. Yet before and after these painting sessions, she was deeply saddened about being unable to die. The bodily symptoms increased, and in effect the time for dying had arrived. Eventually, she said in passing, "If I weren't painting, I would have gone long ago." This comment prompted discussions among the hospice staff, and some persuasion was needed to stop giving the patient her colors because they obstructed her dying process. Following another senseless attack of pain, the team was now prepared to take this step and its consequences. The patient rebelled briefly but then subsided. She lived for one more day, suffering an occasional convulsive back and forth, before dying peacefully.

End-of-life care means allowing a person to die, by following the inner requirements of the dying process. Given what we know about the laws of transition and about the transformation of perception, we should not stimulate the dying (by inducing past stimuli, for instance). Nor should we invite the dying to remain in this world by offering ego-centered opportunities for indulging in the good life. We should refrain from such enticements precisely because the dying actually wish to depart. We must abstain from nurturing their inner contradictions and inconsistencies with well-intended interventions, or by imposing wellness programs, or by exercising too much interdisciplinary know-how. Otherwise, we inevitably risk prolonging life against patients' deep wishes. On the contrary, we must underscore the consequences of lingering. In our palliative care unit (acute-patient ward) it may happen that if patients "come to life again" in our sheltered environment, then at some stage we must tell them that ironclad health insurance regulations compel us to fill in the application forms for a nursing home. Usually such news prompts a change in development. Initially disappointed and utterly depressed, many patients suddenly rediscover their original wish to die and let go, and subsequently most patients die before being discharged. End-of-life care is above all about supporting a process.

THE NEED FOR INDICATION-ORIENTED END-OF-LIFE CARE

Palliative medicine and end-of-life care have become important cornerstones of modern medicine and health care. They are often needs-oriented, and both also give close attention to adequate human communication and to involving all human dimensions (bodily, spiritual, and psychological). And yet, with a view to what occurs within the dying process (the transformation of perception), I urge us to reconsider the present orientation toward patients' verbalized needs. While of course the expressly spoken signals of the dying merit careful consideration, so do their nonverbal signals. And even when that is acknowledged, much remains insufficiently understood. Gathered at a deathbed, we all (relatives, physicians, nursing staff, therapists, and pastoral caregivers) are unable spontaneously to know exactly what a dying person needs. How might we tell a cry for help from a strange bodily phenomenon? Is sedation in the present case appropriate or not? What measures are important, how and when are they to be provided, and which ones are compatible in each individual case? How many visitors, how much rest, how much activity is good for a particular patient? Does the regimen of care produce interferences and complications? Palliative medicine and end-of-life care take great pains to answer these questions on a case-by-case basis. We come closer to a patient's presumed inner reality

by "feeling our way forward" and by leaving such questions open
rather than by jumping to premature conclusions.

A basic knowledge of the dying process of individual as well
as of "archetypal" aspects can serve as a compass for finding our
way within the darkness of the inner experience of the dying
person. Understanding precedes action. This is a sine qua non of
indication-oriented end-of-life care. The concept of changing
perception discussed in this book is precisely part of such basic
knowledge. As such, it can help professionals and laypersons alike
provide more adequate and more competent end-of-life care.
Such a conception contributes to systematically exploring the
inner and spiritual components of complex situations and diffuse
pain, and to better grasping the meaning of certain phenomena
(a peculiar body posture, a gesture) or symbolically charged words.
Standing at a deathbed as a therapist, and realizing that the dying
process is somehow blocked, I ask myself the following questions:

- What remains to be done in this person's life, outwardly and
  inwardly?
- What fear, feeling of forlornness and threat, or catharsis does
  this person still need to go through? Am I encountering a transitional distress or a nameless primordial fear in this patient?
- What does this person still need to integrate (for instance,
  the starving inner child)? Or do a traumatized soul, the great
  achievements as a mother or father, or other important deeds
  in life, still go unacknowledged?
- What does this person still need to let go of? The family, the
  dog? Or, more broadly, ego-centered being and its temptations?
- What does this person still want to find? For instance, primordial trust, connectedness, a spiritual experience or "religio"
  (etymologically, "religion" entails both aspects: *religare* [to tie,

bind], which I sum up with the expression "being connected," and *relegere* [read over again]).

With these questions in mind, I feel my way forward and make observations: What comes toward me from this patient? These observations and impressions I discuss with the attending physicians and nurses. Instead of being a full-blown, maximal procedure, successful end-of-life care needs to be indication-oriented. The question guiding such treatment is less "What does this patient want?" than "What does she or he need?" Do the needs expressed by patients, or those attributed to them, possibly contradict their nonverbal signals or their inner process? And how do we, patient and therapist, or the members of a caregiving team, reach a consensus about what is needed? Besides a sensitive attentiveness to verbal and nonverbal messages, we also need to be aware of *energies* and their orientation (forward, backward, blocked, angry, or flowing). And besides an awareness of peripheral signs, close attention must also be given to the crucial process of transformation and its urging toward one specific goal: that of being able to let go of oneself and die. Indication-oriented means that palliative care has to be an answer to patients' needs and symptoms, as well as to their nonverbalized emotions, longings, and sensitivities, and above all to what is indicated by their outer and inner processes.

MORE OCCURS IN DYING THAN MEETS THE EYE

Dying casts shadows of fear far beyond itself and well in advance. The sight of the dying can sometimes be shocking. At times, relatives are horrified at the unsightliness of a loved one, in particular

if they are mere bystanders to the dying process and to the woe-
ful sight of a loved one: the half-closed eyes, the emaciated body,
the stertorous breathing, the never-ending perseverance. Many
relatives cannot help from casting a furtive glance, only to look
away almost instantly. Surviving relatives often struggle to free
their minds of such images, which may even become traumatic.
"I would never want to die like *that*!" exclaim many people, who
consider receiving active euthanasia later in life. Many advocates
of liberalized death-on-demand often bear the scars of unpro-
cessed trauma (Zimmermann-Acklin 2009:27; see also the right-
to-die advocate Humphry 2002). Struggling to come to terms
with the death of a brother, mother, or even their own child, may
lead others to take up hospice or volunteer work.

Observation, I have noticed, can numb the soul. But sheer
observation (looking at) does not amount to seeing through to
the events and processes actually occurring within the dying
person. What do people concerned with death need to hear?
What perspective might alleviate their fear, encouraging them to
accompany a dying person on their final passage? I would venture
the following answer:

> The suffering of the dying often looks much worse to observers
> than it feels to the person affected. Thus, more happens in dying
> than can be observed from an outer point of view comparable to
> near-death experiences.

Arrival at this viewpoint is a most important consequence of
the model for dying presented in this book. Because of their transformation of perception, inwardly the dying are often elsewhere,
in a neutral or even beautiful, but certainly other, state, one that
is removed from the ego and lies beyond pain and helplessness.

Whereas dying is distressing and full of suffering, it is also a very impressive process that illuminates the meaning of an individual life, an extreme experience par excellence. In dying, as well as in being together with the dying, we draw closer to the uttermost secret of life. We are moved and astonished. The dying teach us much about life, in particular about the laws of living at the margins of existence. It is simply mistaken to consider dying only from the observational perspective of the ego, and its ego functions and sensations, and to imagine oneself lying on a deathbed. Consequently, it is equally often mistaken when visiting a deathbed to transfer the observed suffering onto the dying person and to attribute strong pain to that person (see also Kellehear 2014). The dying are not always fully present when they cry out or suffer from shortness of breath. By no means do I intend to make light of the severe suffering endured at times by the dying. However, when the dying drift away into ego-distant states, removed from everyday consciousness, their sense of suffering also subsides. Their suffering is neither persistent nor coincidental but instead integral with a continuous process of letting go and transformation. It is secondary, I would argue, whether the dying consciously accept their own demise (i.e., let go affirmatively) or unconsciously (vibrational, a tiredness with life). What matters is that the dying find their way into a state beyond pain and fear. Then, if not before, acceptance happens.

DYING WITH DIGNITY

"I don't want to die without dignity." "I don't want my husband to die an undignified death." That is, we resist the idea of dying forsakenly, mercilessly, deprived of visible strength and grace. "I'm like a worm," said a young very ill man. Today, however, "dying with dignity" has become a catchphrase that obscures the question of ultimate human dignity. It is assumed that dignity depends on the autonomous functioning and decision-making capacity of the ego (Pullman 2002; van Brussel 2012). But what, I wonder, if this functioning ego ceases to exist in the passage toward death? What if good dying means, as my work indicates, being able to let go of the ego? I have already discussed the question of dignity in dying, and of the dignity of the dying (chapter 2). The key question is: Is there also dignity in the midst of suffering? Often the dying, in addition to their distress, are also deprived of social appreciation. Current debates on the dignity and indignity of the dying unfortunately lead scores of terminally ill and dying patients to believe they have neither dignity nor worth. "My life is useless now; I feel like garbage to be disposed of," patients often tell me despondently. Thus we need to ask a broader question: Does not dignity apply also to the millions of starving and oppressed people who everyday must fight for survival and for their children's future? What about the dignity of slum children?

A conceptual distinction is needed. Dignity is not attributed only to the autonomous and self-empowered ego, but related moreover to the essence of humankind. The much-touted slogan of dignified dying translates into self-determined dying, often manifesting as the broadly civic claim to decide freely for and about oneself. Dignity and ego-related self-determination, however, are clearly distinct, just as are human rights and entitlement.

The concept of human rights, which marked an important extension of Enlightenment ideals during the second half of the twentieth century, created a new awareness among peoples of the world and their leaders (e.g., the German constitution's commitment to respect fundamental human rights, or President Jimmy Carter's proclamation of human rights). And yet a fundamental human right is not necessarily equal to either a general or a specific entitlement or vanity. Thus the claim to self-determined dying without suffering cannot be equated with the human right of prisoners not to be degraded, humiliated, or turned into sheer objects. Human rights concern the protection of individuals and groups against suffering humiliation at the hands of other people, power structures, and systems. With regard to dying, this would mean that the dying need to be protected against too many interventions. They should never be objects of medical research and machinery (see the concerns of patient directives). By contrast, the demand for self-determined dying concerns what *naturally* emerges at the peripheral dimensions of life, including physical and mental illness, accidents, invalidity, poverty. Dying and creatureliness are fundamental conditions of human existence such as to be begotten and born, which no one can self-determine.

We need to rephrase the question about dignity in suffering and in dying, and ask: What maintains dignity in the midst of suffering? As discussed in chapter 2, the dying person's experience of dignity is the result of:

Dignified treatment. Such treatment reminds patients of their intrinsic value. While smiling at me, Mrs. Spinnler was interrupted by an attack of pain. "Ach . . ." The treatment, she reassured me, was first-rate: The care provided afforded her self-esteem.

The human capacity to not simply succumb to one's humiliating situation, and to keep one's own identity, even in the midst of suffering or following a stroke of fate. If we are capable of establishing an inner relationship to our suffering and the accompanying degrading circumstances, then we are more than our illness or desolate situation. This dignity empowers us to react in a responsible (and responsive) manner. Dignity, under such circumstances, is thus sometimes described as the inner power of endurance. Then we still experience ourselves as a subject even in suffering. "I have never been myself the way I am now," a fully conscious half-paralyzed patient told me. Another patient, a thirty-year-old father nearing death, said: "One day, I would like my daughter to know who her father was." He kept a diary in which he recorded his everyday experiences for her sake: what eating meant to him, how he felt being guided out into the park in his wheelchair, what his feelings were whenever he saw his little daughter. Both patients meaningfully exerted their subjectivity against their suffering. Dignity therapy as developed by Harvey Chochinov and his colleagues (2005) and maturation described for instance by Richard Rohr (2011) help to attain such a sense of dignity and to keep one's own identity.

The inviolability of human dignity (Kant). Before me sat a mother whose posture was conspicuously upright, yet who was descending into confusion as a result of brain metastases. Her husband explained to me what his wife no longer understood and how he was running a household with five children. His wife was mostly unable to follow his words, except here and there, when she added: "Yes, that's how it is." She was moved when I praised her for the dignity she was expressing despite her lack of understanding. "I believe there is something that I shall never lose," she remarked coherently.

The most important challenge when dealing with confused or demented patients is not to let symptoms, physical appearance, or social barriers dissuade us from granting such persons dignity. "I rarely visit my demented sister," said one young woman. "It seems more important to hold together within myself the fragments of her mental being. I feel an inner urge, not to stop believing in her dignity. My impression is that my sister perceives this." Taking this idea to its logical conclusion, dignity is what remains mysteriously present and stands above us, despite the disintegration of body and mind.

Dignity needs to be seen as distinct from vanity. It is not the acclaim or reverence derived from worldly things such as status, reputation, or achievement, but by contrast dignity is a counterquality to embarrassment. Where exactly does embarrassment begin? Curiously, nature and the animal kingdom have no sense of embarrassment. As if animals or plants could not fail to achieve their entelechy in quite the same way as the human being endowed with free will. Embarrassment springs from the self-alienated, divided human being unaware of his or her alienation. I feel embarrassed, for instance, when a dying patient, fully aware of her condition but without any outer necessity, asks to be driven to a beauty salon or to the dentist's three days before her death. Or if a dying millionaire is still counting his millions on his deathbed. "Doesn't he get it?" one wonders. Sheer creatureliness, however, is not embarrassing. Children, as long as they are not narcissistically alienated from themselves, are not embarrassing. This is equally true of elderly or ill persons. Their radiance has less to do with their more or less intact reasoning than with their emotional wholeness. Dignity exists when individuals do not lag behind themselves, nor behind the natural challenge presented by the suffering. Dignity is a relational term (reverence). Usually, it results from a relationship between two persons. But behind this interpersonal level, dignity stems from an invisible relationship between a human being and God, the divine, a supernatural being, a higher power. Dignity is a hallmark of civilized humanity.

The fierce social debate about dignity and indignity, dying and self-determination, plainly suggests that much is at stake. Dying as a cultural asset is under threat. We are challenged to restore dignity to dying processes—that is, to treat with deference the magnitude and significance of this final act in the drama that is human life. The dying wish their language to be recognized. The natural extreme experience of death consists of an intrinsic intensity of sensuality, tenderness, love, and spirituality (Kellehear 2014; Kuhl 2002).

Also endangered is respect for the suffering. Dorothee Sölle (1993) argues that emotional numbness and an insensitivity to suffering are becoming increasingly widespread. Also endangered is the atmosphere in hospitals: it is not unusual for health-care professionals to feel dictated by the limit-call for self-determination and assisted suicide. As practitioners, we have ceased being as free as we once were in performing solid professional work.

Generally, then, the overall threat is to the dialogic approach to tensions: If enduring difficult situations and experiences of suffering is no longer esteemed, and if endurance is no longer practiced, then our social, cultural, and intellectual capacities to cope with "the unresolvable" in the world get diminished. Tensions are not always meant to be resolved. Indeed, maintaining tension and differentiating the factors in a charged atmosphere may serve to achieve mature solutions and genuine reconciliation. In a personal conversation about euthanasia, Thomas Cerny, an oncologist and the chief physician at St. Gallen Cantonal Hospital, remarked: "We must endure the existential dilemma and not make physicians into executioners."

Under threat also is our social capacity for relatedness and responsibility. If we view the world increasingly from our ego-centered perspective, we lose our openness toward, and our ability to be affected by, other people and other dimensions—that is, our capacity not only to act but also to receive and to leave matters as such. Relatedness, ultimately, is not an act of volition aspired to and willed by the ego. Instead it involves allowing for deeper attachment, an inner flowing versus a dissociation from responsibility, connection versus disconnection, an attitude of concern and reliance versus glory and narcissism.

Under particular threat is the older generation. The debate about self-determined dying and euthanasia concerns more and more patient populations, perhaps especially patients with mental disorders or elderly persons. Elderly and frail persons often come to feel useless and a burden for their families and society because we normally do not value maturation and old age.

Under threat, finally, is our respect for mystery and for our state of ultimately not knowing. In religious terms, so-called self-determined dying leads to losing our awe of God; in ontological terms, to losing our respect for the incomprehensibility of being and the existent. Our sense of mystery is waning. Conversely, respect and awe bring forth a new—searching, marveling, praying—openness toward the incomprehensible. Socrates's insight, "I know that I know nothing," leads us consistently, and from within ourselves, away from a glorification of the ego, toward and into sustained existential uncertainty. Socrates, who sought the truth until his last breath, drank the cup of poison not of his own choosing but because he was sentenced to death for his purported ungodliness. He refused to escape or to ask for mercy. Taking the cup, and holding it to his mouth with steady hands, he was supposed to have said: "We can and must pray to the gods that our sojourn on earth will continue happy beyond the grave. This is my prayer, and may it come to pass" (Plato 1914 [*Phaedo*]). No sooner had he uttered these words than he stoically drank the potion.

ESCHATOLOGY AND MYSTERY

The question of the whereupon of life and creation occupies an important role in both the Hebrew Bible and the New Testament, just as among other peoples, religions, and their conceptions of existence. Here, I want to list some final questions every dying patient deals with, consciously or unconsciously. Once again, let me mention that followers of the different religions and traditions may complete this list of questions: Do we find our way back to paradise, near God, near Allah, to the cycle of nature, to heaven, or instead to nothing? Do we reach nirvana? Will there be a rebirth or a kingdom of God? Will Israel witness the restoration of the old social order, as prophesized in Micah 5? Will a ruler of peace come, as Isaiah (9, 11) suggests? Will the dead be resurrected (1 Cor. 15)? How, then, should the Christian dying conceive resurrection and Parousia (the coming of Christ, as written in 1 Thess. 2:19, 3:13, 4:15, 5:23; 1 Cor. 15:23; 2 Pet. 3:4, etc.)? Will there be any order or higher power which will perfect and judge the world and the souls?

Eschatology is that branch of Christian theology that envisages the end-time of creation and history, and the destiny of humanity. Many eminent German-speaking theologians were and still are attracted to eschatology in their later years and have been eager to discuss the subject (Jüngel and Ferrario 2009; Rahner 2004). And yet the final questions in life remain open. Individuals and traditions give different answers. Besides the question of truth, the material of the holy scriptures of the different religions, of myth and folktales has a deep archetypal and symbolic meaning. Dying—still—ends in mystery.

From a psychological viewpoint, there are three aspects of the "beyond":

1. The question of *forward or backward*.

Does dying close the cycle of being by leading us back to the beginning, to participation in being, and to God, the Whole, a Supreme Being, or a higher power? Or does dying instead lead us forward, into participating in a *new* and novel dimension of being, of God, and/or of the Supreme Being? Also implicit here, aside from the matter of varying worldviews, is the question of whether God or the Supreme Being also evolve , as substance (plenitude and emptiness) and as energy (see, e.g., process theology [Keller 2008]). Assuming a difference between the primordial state and the final state of creation, we may venture to infer that the Whole, or God is, to put it boldly, "in flux, and in becoming."[1] If the primordial and final states are not identical, then divine perfection must be reconceived accordingly, not in terms of immutable perfection but rather of a comprehensive, dynamic whole.

2. The mystical question of *relationship versus being*.

Is the Supreme Being, is God, or is the Whole, ultimately also perceived in terms of relationship or of being? Does dying ultimately lead to a relationship (I–Thou), or to a state of being, or to both: a union of relationship and being, a form of ultimate relatedness, and "unio mystica"?

3. The question of meaning.

Do we believe in a higher order or does finally nothing—sheer coincidence—remain?

The answers to these questions weigh heavily. They decide whether we may assign an ultimate meaningfulness to ourselves and to all life and love or not. They determine whether the pains we take to attain awareness and maturation ultimately have positive consequences. Meaning or sheer coincidence—those are the alternatives. There is no in-between.

If we assume that the whole has an ultimate meaning, and that there is an ultimate relatedness and participation, then human development is not simply exhausted by an individual life (destiny) reaching its end. As human beings, we are involved in a larger becoming, in life as in death. This can be conceived in terms of religion or not. We are, to borrow a wonderful Hebrew Bible image, part of a nation that includes all the nations that go forth to the sacred mountain (Mic. 4:1–5). It remains open when and how fulfillment occurs on this path. The reactions of many dying persons from different religious backgrounds suggest that what we go toward in the dying process also contains fulfillment. Their vision of final events is limited neither to the historical (time-bound) nor to their individual suffering nor to the present. Instead, it must be understood as the simultaneity of past, present, and future, of individual experience and archetypal spiritual dimensions, of suffering and redemption. What changes concretely are the following nine points:

1. The aspect of time, temporality, present, and presence (Lommel 2010): much suggests a mode of being characterized by simultaneity and timelessness.

2. The aspect of space, spatiality: much suggests unboundedness and eternity.

3. Body sensations, embodiments, delimitation, boundedness, and identity of the self: much suggests an infinite relatedness and being per se. My image for this state is our partaking of being, of God, of substance, and of energy. This substance can be either plenitude or emptiness.

4. The sense of gravity and of bodily heaviness seems to fall into a state of weightlessness.

5. Intensity, sensuousness: intensity seems to intensify (see also Kellehear 2014). Sensuousness and a state beyond the senses coincidence.

6. Divisions, ambivalences, dissociations, and also value judge-
   ments such as good and evil become superfluous or are under-
   pinned by the whole. Development points from the particular
   to the whole.

7. Awareness: from unconsciousness and ego-bound consciousness to a new kind of "seeing," "partaking," a new kind of consciousness (Rohr 2009).

8. Energy: from the urging and waiting to the fulfilled, from
   seeking to finding, from struggle to peace.

9. From the individual to holy community and feast (imagined,
   for instance, as the holy city on the mountain, as the new
   Jerusalem, as a new paradise, or a new eon), from the individual
   to the (holy) community and feast (e.g., holy wedding).

Whether the testimonies of the dying are interpreted as a revelation of afterlife or just as an end-of-life experience (Fenwick
and Brayne 2011) and/or a near-death experience remain open.
This is a matter of personal judgment. The process of dying moves
us toward a mysterious apex (Kuhl 2002). Nevertheless we die
our very own deaths. Some become like a child finding the great
trust beyond all fear. Others, perhaps jesters all their life, smile
amused at the all-too-human events surrounding the deathbed.
Their ingenuousness is their greatness. Dying, they flit across to
the other side, quite unexpectedly, and thus play one last trick
on their relatives. Others die quietly and close to reality, stoically.
Others "experience" and live through, in the true sense of the
word, the invisible transition to uttermost maturation and truth,
and thus become a sage or a mystic.

Those of us gathered at the deathbed remain behind in two
ways: (1) we survive the deceased, and (2) even if we look toward

the mystery we cannot partake in it. And we are left to our sense of reality, which forbids ecstatic embellishment and reminds us of our limits and limitations. Yet we are also left astonished, marveling at what the dying, and their transition, teach us. We die as a child, a fool, a realist, or a mystic.

EPILOGUE

Finding Home

We all find our way home
And yet none of us will be right.
Each of us falls into trust,
into his or her God.
We are all revered, as if chastened,
related in being
full and empty,
blessed and serene.

MONIKA RENZ

APPENDIX

PATIENTS, OCCURRENCE OF THEMES, AND FACTORS

Themes	Pilot study (80 patients)	Follow-up study (600 patients)
Transition confirmed as a process	38 (48%)	149 (25%)
Spiritual opening/post-transition	43 (54%)	305 (51%)
Information about transition helps relatives		335 (56%)
Anxiety		397 (66%)
Fear of dying/uncertainty	11 (14%)	61 (10%)
Fear of pain/powerlessness	28 (35%)	302 (50%)
Angst as part of transition	30 (38%)	261 (44%)
Fear of being alone in dying	15 (19%)	
Struggle within transition	24 (30%)	180 (30%)
Acceptance	55 (69%)	541 (90%)
From anger to acceptance	24 (30%)	272 (45%)
Prolonged denial	13 (16%)	198 (33%)

(*Continued*)

PATIENTS, OCCURRENCE OF THEMES, AND FACTORS

Themes	Pilot study (80 patients)	Follow-up study (600 patients)
Total denial of death	6 (8%)	
Just ready/ripe to die	12 (15%)	71 (12%)
Relatives important	66 (82%)	466 (78%)
Need to settle severe family problems	25 (31%)	155 (26%)
Family members important, but not near death	41 (51%)	311 (52%)
Maturation		374 (62%)
Life review	37 (46%)	292 (49%)
Trauma	15 (19%)	122 (20%)
Individuation, meaning of life	25 (31%)	181 (30%)

Note: Demographics (age range; sex): pilot study: 27–84; 43 females, 37 males; follow-up study: 21–86; 307 females, 292 males.

Source: Renz, Schuett Mao, Bueche, Cerny, and Strasser (2013).

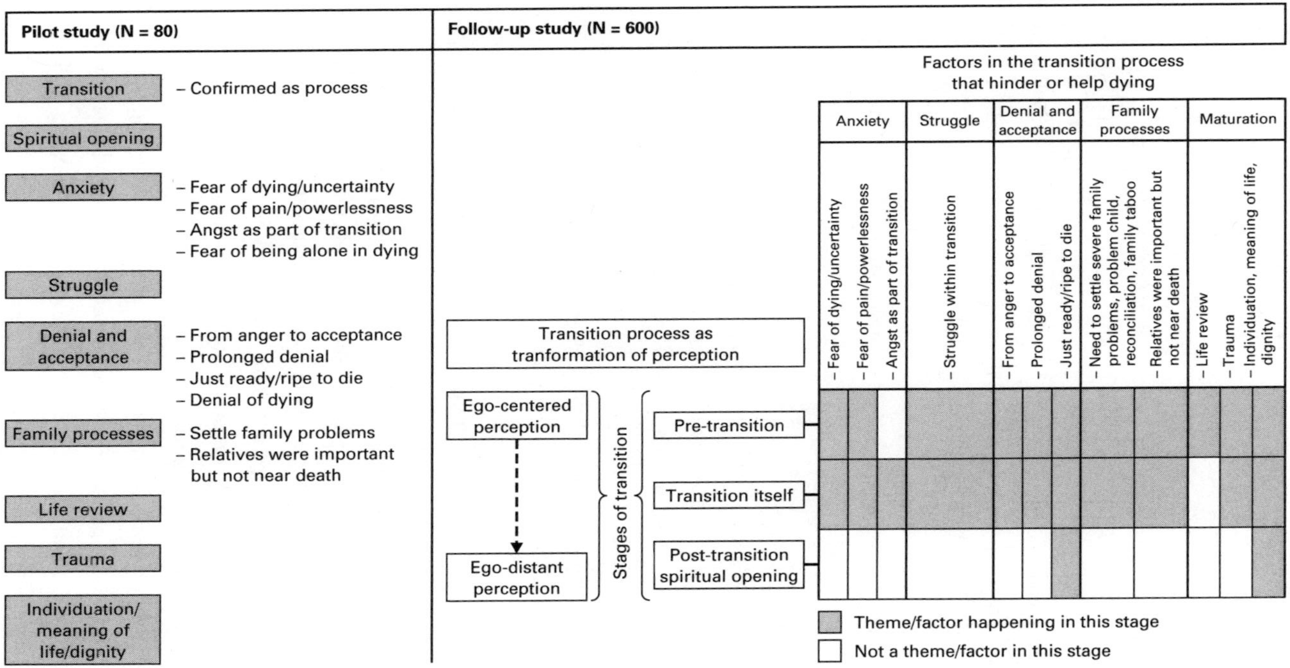

FIGURE A.1 Table of themes. (From Renz, Schuett Mao, Bueche, Cerny, and Strasser 2013)

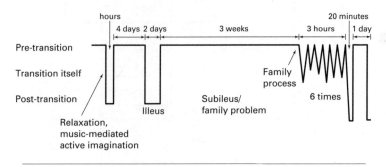

FIGURE A.2 Case vignette patient 1: Andrew Adam. (From Renz et al. 2013)

Andrew Adam, with progressing urothelium carcinoma, had severe local pain. Medically, it was not clear why he could not die for a long time and why he suddenly passed away. He had huge family problems. His wife was going to have a physical check-up. Eight days prior to this date, he was willing to try a relaxation exercise and a *Klangreise* (music-assisted active imagination). After the intervention, he was relaxed for hours and quiet, as if mentally far away. Later, he told us that he felt serene and had no pain.

Four days later, I heard that he was terminally diagnosed with an ileus. He nodded when I asked him whether he felt serene, but otherwise he remained in an uncommunicative state for two days, even in the presence of his relatives. When his wife's check-up was brought up, he immediately became awake. The ileus had developed into a subileus.

Three weeks later, when he accepted his fate, giving up his demand for physician-assisted suicide, and after finding a way to resolve unsettled family matters, he became terminal again. For three hours, he was in transition.

He was afraid of falling and desperately clutched at the bed frame. I held his hand in mine and interpreted his fear. He relaxed. Then he became anxious and restless again. I told him, "You are safe." He relaxed. He then moved his feet around, as if pushing off from the bed. I put my hands up, giving his feet resistance, and encouraged him to continue. He followed my instruction and calmed down again. He had a rapt, wondering expression on his face. Serenity—Then he cried out as if actually threatened. I interpreted for him the feeling of threat. This obviously alleviated his fear. I blessed him and said that many biblical quotes mentioned a crowd of angels overpowering darkness. He relaxed, got a serene expression on his face, and uttered "Flowers."

Twenty minutes later, he was alert again, disappointed because he had not yet died. For the night, he was given a sedative medication. The next day, he conveyed that it had been beautiful "over there." The following night, he died peacefully.

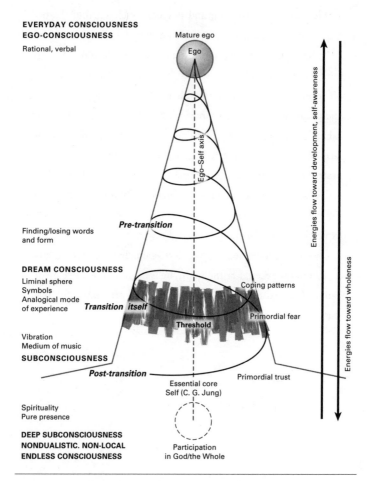

FIGURE A.3 States of consciousness. (Renz 2011/2015)

NOTES

INTRODUCTION

1. At St. Gallen Cantonal Hospital, Switzerland, patients experiencing distressing multidimensional symptoms, which are identified by physicians, nurses, and therapists and which are not controllable in a waking state, receive sedation just for one night in the first instance (in addition to symptom specific medication, for instance, haloperidol for delirium or morphine for dyspnea). The next day, the sedation and its effects are discussed. Often temporary sedation, including phases when patients are awake, is sufficient. Unlike other approaches, this approach to sedation does not severely interrupt family or therapeutic-spiritual processes (Dr. Daniel Büche, Dr. Florian Strasser, Dr. Thomas Cerny). Approaching death, as I have observed elsewhere, patients need less and less sedation, even if they have many symptoms (Renz, Schuett Mao, Bueche, Cerny, and Strasser 2013).

2. Twice a year, I co-teach such an education program with Daniel Büche, a specialist in palliative medicine. The program is aimed at physicians, nurses, therapists, chaplains, social workers, and interested lay persons (e.g., relatives, close friends). It includes lectures on dying as a transition, discussions of case vignettes and near-death experiences, analysis of the symbols occurring in folktales, and firsthand experience with music-assisted relaxation.

3. Here the question arises whether my own spirituality affects interpretation. I am an open-minded religious person and a practicing
Christian, and am attracted to the combination of religion; depth psychology of Carl Jung, Erich Neumann, and Stanislav Grof; and music
therapy. Impressed by many encounters with patients, after some years
of practice in psycho-oncology, I decided to broaden my background
and studied theology at the universities of Zurich (Protestant), Innsbruck, and Fribourg (Catholic). I am also influenced by my studies
in ethno-musicology, where I focused on healing rituals in different
ethnic groups. I often have in-depth discussions and conversations
with agnostics, who are not adverse to discussions of my approach to
religion (Renz 2008a, 2013), to human development, and to dying (see
figure A.3). My deepest formative experiences occurred during bouts
of illness when I was young and later after several accidents. What I
experienced was similar to a near-death experience and enhanced my
sensitivity (e.g., for music and vibration). My patients' deathbed visions
and near-death experiences have influenced my special approach to
theology, as several theologians agree: I differentiate three paths of
interpretation of various holy scriptures such as the Bible: (1) there are
words of revelation, written by humans inspired by a holy spirit; and
(2) there are passages that have to be interpreted from a historical-
critical perspective because they are influenced decisively by their
historical context. These two approaches are common, but a third
approach has to be taken into account: (3) passages have to be interpreted on an (archetypal and/or culturally bound) symbolic level that
corresponds to dream consciousness more than to rational everyday
consciousness (see figure A.3). When these scriptures were written,
people lived and thought naturally in terms of symbols and metaphors.
Exactly this symbolical world seems to be analogous to the experiences
and metaphors of the dying. Knowing about them helps caregivers to
better understand the specific language of patients. Otherwise patients
wait and wait to be understood. Nonetheless, it is important in all
end-of-life care to raise the question of bias again and again (see the
discussion of the limitations of my research in the section "Methodology and Background Research" and in chapter 3, note 3).

4. All the patients discussed in this book had advanced cancer. Their names have been changed, and their personal data anonymized, to protect their privacy.

2. THE THREE STAGES OF TRANSITION AND DIGNITY

1. In this folktale, a girl sits at a spinning wheel and spins all day until she hurts her finger and the spindle gets bloody. She wants to wash the spindle, but it falls into the well. Her stepmother demands that she jump down the well to fetch the spindle. She finds herself in a meadow, full of sunshine and beautiful flowers. She comes to an oven full of baked bread, to a tree full of ripe apples, and to the little house of the great Mother Hulda (an archetypal mother). There she does the housework and gets enough good food. After a longer or shorter time in the underworld, which is beyond time and space, she gets homesick even if she has a better life in the underworld. Mother Hulda guides her back to the gate to the upperworld and gives her back the spindle and lots of gold. Her sister also wants to have the gold but is insensitive to the underworld and its rules. Standing under the gate, the sister isn't showered with gold but covered with sticky pitch. The two girls are called Gold Mary and Pitch Mary. See "Mother Hulda," *Grimms' Fairy Tales*, http://www.grimmstories.com/en/grimm_fairy-tales/mother_hulda (accessed December 5, 2014).

3. WHAT IS PRIMORDIAL FEAR?

1. In German, "Das Ich stirbt in ein Du hinein" is an important concept, which corresponds to Martin Buber's (1923/1937) phrase "I become through my relation to the *Thou*" (11). It is the most wanted title of my lectures for any audience of up to two thousand listeners (more than five hundred times so far).

2. Quadriplegics are unable to move any parts of their body, in contrast to paraplegics, who can move their arms but not their legs.

3. For my use of the term "God" in such situations, see also the example of Alfred Armbruster (introduction). "God" is a word that is frequently understood. It stands for the inner experience of a numinous dimension, which can deeply touch and overwhelm patients, even those without faith and religion. They all need guidance. I have no intention of converting them to any concept of God but instead try to help patients to relate their inner experiences. The symbol of the eye is crucial in these experiences and is especially fear-evoking (e.g., "dragon" etymologically stands for the sharp-eyed, in German *der Scharfblickende*). I quite often recognize this phenomenon in patients. They cannot understand what is happening to them (see also the case of Simona and the following case narratives). After my lectures, I am often told that other professionals also observe the phenomenon but have so far found no interpretation. There is an urgent need to discuss this phenomenon because it seems to be one of our deepest taboo subjects. I call it primordial fear, which is encompassed by primordial trust, into which patients eventually fall and feel redeemed, safe, and peaceful.

4. "The Goose-Girl at the Well," *Grimms' Fairy Tales*, http://www .grimmstories.com/en/grimm_fairy-tales/the_goose_girl_at_the_well (accessed December 5, 2014).

5. "The Girl Without Hands," *Grimms' Fairy Tales*, http://www .grimmstories.com/en/grimm_fairy-tales/the_girl_without_hands (accessed December 5, 2014).

7. DYING WITH DIGNITY

1. In German, *im Werden*; God is also one who is "becoming" (*ein Werdender*), as I have explained elsewhere (Renz 2009:281–282, 2013:134–135). See also Karl Rahner's avowal: "God not only *is*, but can also *become*" (Gott *ist* nicht nur, sondern kann auch *werden*) (quoted in Klinger 1994:41). Modern process theology pursues a similar idea (Keller 2008).

REFERENCES

Archie, P., Bruera, E., and Cohen, L. (2013). Music-based interventions in palliative cancer care: A review of quantitative studies and neurobiological literature. *Supportive Care in Cancer* 21 (9):2609–2624.

Arnold, B. L., and Lloyd, L. S. (2013). Harnessing complex emergent metaphors for effective communication in palliative care: A multimodal perceptual analysis of hospice patients' reports of transcendence experiences. *American Journal of Hospice and Palliative Medicine* 31 (3):292–299.

Balboni, T. A., Paulk, M. E., Balboni, M. J., Phelps, A. C., Loggers, E. T., Wright, A. A., et al. (2010). Provision of spiritual care to patients with advanced cancer: Associations with medical care and quality of life near death. *Journal of Clinical Oncology* 28 (3):445–452.

Becker, H., and Geer, B. (2004). Participant observation and interviewing: A comparison. In C. Seale (Ed.), *Social research methods: A reader* (246–251). London: Routledge.

Bible (1997). Authorized King James Version. Oxford: Oxford University Press.

Bluebond-Langner, M., Belasco, J. B., Goldman, A., and Belasco, C. (2007). Understanding parents' approaches to care and treatment of children with cancer when standard therapy has failed. *Journal of Clinical Oncology* 25 (17):2414–2419.

Breitbart, W., Rosenfeld, B., Gibson, C., Pessin, H., Poppito, S., Nelson, C., et al. (2010). Meaning-centered group psychotherapy for patients with advanced cancer: A pilot randomized controlled trial. *Psychoncology* 19 (1):21–28.

Bruno, M. A., Ledoux, D., and Laureys, S. (2009). The dying human: A perspective from biomedicine. In A. Kellehear (Ed.), *The study of dying: From autonomy to transformation* (51–76). Cambridge: Cambridge University Press.

Buber, M. (1923/1937). *I and thou.* (R. G. Smith, Trans.). Edinburgh: Clark.

Byock, I. (1997). *Dying well: The prospect for growth at the end of life.* New York: Riverhead.

Chochinov, H. M., Hack, T., Hassard, T., Kristjanson, L. J., McClement, S., and Harlos, M. (2005). Dignity therapy: A novel psychotherapeutic intervention for patients near the end of life. *Journal of Clinical Oncology* 23 (24):5520–5525.

Corr, C. A. (1991–1992). A task-based approach to coping with dying. *Omega* 24:81–94.

Corr, C. A., Doka, K. J., and Kastenbaum, R. (1999). Dying and its interpreters: A review of selected literature and some comments on the state of the field. *Omega* 39 (4):239–259.

Drewermann, E. (1985). *Tiefenpsychologie und Exegese.* Vol. 2, *Die Wahrheit der Werke und der Worte: Wunder, Vision, Weissagung, Apokalypse, Geschichte, Gleichnis.* Olten: Walter Verlag.

Drewermann, E. (1987). *Das Markusevangelium: Bilder von Erlösung.* 2 vols. Olten: Walter Verlag.

Drewermann, E. (1989). *Tiefenpsychologie und Exegese.* Vol. 1, *Die Wahrheit der Formen: Traum, Mythos, Märchen, Sage und Legende* (7th ed.). Olten: Walter Verlag.

Fenwick, P., and Brayne, S. (2011). End-of-life experiences: Reaching out for compassion, communication, and connection-meaning of deathbed visions and coincidences. *American Journal of Hospice and Palliative Care* 28 (1):7–15.

Fenwick, P., and Fenwick, E. (2008). *The art of dying: A journey to elsewhere.* London: Continuum.

Finlay, L., and Evans, K. (Eds.). (2009). *Relational-centred research for psychotherapists: Exploring meanings and experience.* Malden, Mass.: Wiley-Blackwell.

Gaeta, S., and Price, K. J. (2010). End-of-life issues in critically ill cancer patients. *Critical Care Clinics* 26 (1):219–227.

Grimm, J., and Grimm, W. (1984). *Kinder- und Hausmärchen: Gesammelt durch die Brüder Grimm.* 3 vols. Frankfurt: Insel.

Grof, S., and Grof, C. (1984). *Jenseits des Todes.* Stuttgart: Kösel.

Holloway, M., Adamson, S., McSherry, W., and Swinton, J. (2011). Spiritual care at the end of life: A systematic review of the literature. https://www.gov.uk/government/uploads/system/uploads/attachment_data/file/215798/dh_123804.pdf (accessed June 2, 2014).

Humphry, D. (2002). *Final exit: The practicalities of self-deliverance and assisted suicide for the dying* (3rd ed.). New York: Delta Trade.

James, W. (1902/2010). *The varieties of religious experience.* Library of America Paperback Classics. New York: Library of America.

Jüngel, E., and Ferrario, F. (Eds.) (2009). *Die Leidenschaft, Gott zu denken: Ein Gespräch über Denk- und Lebenserfahrungen.* Zurich: Theologischer Verlag.

Kant, I. (1956). *Werke in sechs Bänden.* Vol. 2, *Kritik der reinen Vernunft.* Wiesbaden: Insel.

Kastenbaum, R. J. (2012). *Death, society, and human experience* (11th ed.). Boston: Pearson.

Kearney, M. (1996). *Mortally wounded: Stories of soul pain, death, and healing.* New York: Scribner.

Kellehear, A. (2014). *The inner life of the dying person.* New York: Columbia University Press.

Keller, C. (2008). *On the mystery: Discerning divinity in process.* Minneapolis: Fortress Press.

Klinger, E. (1994). *Das absolute Geheimnis im Alltag entdecken: Zur spirituellen Theologie Karl Rahners.* Würzburg: Echter.

Koenig, B. A., Back, A. L., and Crawley, L. M. (2003). Qualitative methods in end-of-life research: Recommendations to enhance the protection of human subjects. *Journal of Pain and Symptom Management* 25 (4):43–52.

Kübler-Ross, E. (1974). *On death and dying.* New York: Macmillan.

Kuhl, D. (2002). *What dying people want: Practical wisdom for the end of life.* New York: Public Affairs.

Lommel, P. van. (2010). *Consciousness beyond life: The science of the near-death experience.* New York: HarperOne.

Long, J., and Perry, P. (2010). *Evidence of the afterlife: The science of near-death experiences.* New York: HarperOne.

Moody, R. (1988). *The light beyond*. London: Macmillan.

Nahm, M., Greyson, B., and Kelly, E. W. (2012). Terminal lucidity: A review and a case collection. *Archives of Gerontology and Geriatrics* 55 (1):138–142.

Neumann, E. (1963). *Das Kind: Struktur und Dynamik der werdenden Persönlichkeit*. Zurich: Rhein.

Neumann, E. (1983). *Amor und Psyche Deutung eines Märchens: Ein Beitrag zur seelischen Entwicklung des Weiblichen* (4th ed.). Olten: Walter.

Nissim, R., Freeman, E., Lo, C., Zimmerman, C., Gagliese, L., Rydall, A., et al. (2012). Managing Cancer and Living Meaningfully (CALM): A qualitative study of a brief individual psychotherapy for individuals with advanced cancer. *Palliative Medicine* 26 (5):713–721.

Nouwen, H. J. M. (1998). *Die innere Stimme der Liebe*. Freiburg: Herder.

Olson, K. L., Morse, J. M., Smith, J. E., Mayan, M. J., and Hammond, D. (2000–2001). Linking trajectories of illness and dying. *Omega* 42 (4):293–308.

Otto, R. (1917/1987). *Das Heilige: Über das Irrationale in der Idee des Göttlichen und sein Verhältnis zum Rationalen*. Beck'sche Reihe 328. Munich: Beck.

Pantilat, S. Z. (2009). Communicating with seriously ill patients: Better words to say. *Journal of the American Medical Association* 301 (12):1279–1281.

Parnia, S. (2008). *What happens when we die : A ground-breaking study into the nature of life and death* (2nd ed.). London: Hay House.

Patton, J. F. (2006). Jungian spirituality: A developmental context for late-life growth. *American Journal of Hospice and Palliative Medicine* 23 (4):304–308.

Pellegrino E. D. (2002). Professionalism, profession, and the virtues of the good physician. *Mount Sinai Journal of Medicine* 69 (6):378–384.

Plato (1914). *Euthyphro, Apology, Crito, Phaedo, Phaedrus*. (Harold North Fowler, Trans.). Loeb Classical Library 36. Cambridge, Mass.: Harvard University Press.

Puchalski, C. M. (2012). Spirituality in the cancer trajectory. *Annals of Oncology* 23 (suppl. 3):49–55.

Pullman, D. (2002). Human dignity and the ethics and aesthetics of pain and suffering. *Theoretical Medicine and Bioethics* 23 (1):75–94.

Rahner, K. (1982). *Praxis des Glaubens: Geistliches Lesebuch*. (K. Lehmann and A. Raffelt, Eds.). Zurich.: Benziger.

Rahner, K. (2000). Experiences of a Catholic theologian. (D. Marmion and
G. Thiessen, Trans.). *Theological Studies* 61 (1):3–15.

Rahner, K. (2004). *Beten mit Karl Rahner*. Vol. 1, *Von der Not und dem Segen des
Gebetes*. Freiburg: Herder.

Renz, M. (2007). *Von der Chance, wesentlich zu werden: Reflexionen zu Spiritualität, Reifung und Sterben*. Paderborn: Junfermann.

Renz, M. (2008a). *Erlösung aus Prägung: Botschaft und Leben Jesu als Über-
windung der menschlichen Angst-, Begehrens- und Machtstruktur*. Paderborn: Junfermann.

Renz, M. (2000/2008b). *Zeugnisse Sterbender: Todesnähe als Wandlung und
letzte Reifung* (rev., 4th ed.). Paderborn: Junfermann.

Renz, M. (2009). *Zwischen Urangst und Urvertrauen: Aller Anfang ist Über-
gang. Musik, Symbol und Spiritualität in der therapeutischen Arbeit* (enlarged
new ed.). Paderborn: Junfermann.

Renz, M. (2003/2010). *Grenzerfahrung Gott: Spirituelle Erfahrungen in Leid
und Krankheit*. Freiburg: Kreuz.

Renz, M. (2013). *Der Mystiker aus Nazaret: Jesus neu begegnen. Jesuanische Spiritualität*. Freiburg: Kreuz.

Renz, M. (2011/2015). *Hinübergehen: Was beim Sterben geschieht: Annäherungen
an letzte Wahrheiten unseres Lebens*. Freiburg: Kreuz.

Renz, M., Schuett Mao, M., Bueche, D., Cerny, T., and Strasser, F. (2013).
Dying is a transition. *American Journal of Hospice and Palliative Care* 30
(3):283–290.

Renz, M., Schuett Mao, M., Omlin, A., Bueche, D., Cerny, T., and Strasser,
F. (2015). Spiritual experiences of transcendence in patients with advanced
cancer. *American Journal of Hospice and Palliative Medicine* 32 (2):178–188.

Riedel, I. (1978). Das Mädchen des Schmieds, das zu schweigen verstand. In
M. Jakoby, V. Kast, and I. Riedel (Eds.), *Das Böse im Märchen* (130–158).
Fellbach: Bonz.

Riedel, I. (1989). *Die weise Frau in uralt-neuen Erfahrungen: Der Archetyp der
alten Weisen im Märchen und seinem religionsgeschichtlichen Hintergrund*.
Olten: Walter.

Rohr, R. (2009). *The naked now: Learning to see as the mystics see*. New York:
Crossroad.

Rohr, R. (2011). *Falling upward: A spirituality for the two halves of life*. San Francisco: Jossey-Bass.

Rosenzweig, F. (1984). *Der Mensch und sein Werk. Gesammelte Schriften*. Vol. 3, *Zweistromland: Kleinere Schriften zu Glauben und Denken*. (R. Mayer and A. Mayer, Eds.). Dordrecht: Nijhoff.

Samarel, N. (1995). The dying process. In H. Wass and R. A. Neimeyer (Eds.), *Dying: Facing the facts*. Washington, D.C.: Taylor and Francis.

Sand, L., Strang, P., and Milberg, A. (2008). Dying cancer patients' experiences of powerlessness and helplessness. *Supportive Care in Cancer* 16 (7):853–862.

Schroeder-Sheker, T. (2007). Subtle signs of the deathbed vigil: Responding to hearing-impaired, comatose, and vegetative patients. *Explore* 3 (5):517–520.

Shinebourne, P., and Smith, J. A. (2010). The communicative power of metaphors: An analysis and interpretation of metaphors in accounts of the experience of addiction. *Psychology and Psychotherapy* 83 (pt. 1):59–73.

Smith, J. A., Flowers, P., and Larkin, M. (2009). *Interpretative phenomenological analysis: Theory, method, and research*. Thousand Oaks, Calif.: Sage.

Smith, T. J., Temin, S., Alesi, E. R., Abernethy, A. P., Balboni, T. A., Basch, E. M., et al. (2012). American Society of Clinical Oncology provisional clinical opinion: The integration of palliative care into standard oncology care. *Journal of Clinical Oncology* 30 (8):880–887.

Sölle, D. (1993). *Leiden*. Freiburg: Herder.

Steinhauser, K. E., and Barroso, J. (2009). Using qualitative methods to explore key questions in palliative care. *Journal of Palliative Medicine* 12 (8):725–730.

Strasser, F., Walker, P., and Bruera, E. (2005). Palliative pain management: When both pain and suffering hurt. *Journal of Palliative Care* 21 (2):69–79.

Strobel, W., and Huppmann, G. (Eds.). (1991). *Musiktherapie: Grundlagen, Formen, Möglichkeiten* (2nd ed.). Göttingen: Hogrefe.

Tomatis, A. (1987). *Der Klang des Lebens vorgeburtliche Kommunikation, die Anfänge der seelischen Entwicklung*. Reinbek bei Hamburg: Rowohlt.

Tomer, A., Eliason, G., and Wong, P. T. P. (Eds.). (2008). *Existential and spiritual issues in death attitudes*. New York: Erlbaum.

Turner, V. W. (1969). *The ritual process: Structure and anti-structure*. London: Routledge and Kegan Paul.

Van Brussel, L. (2012). Autonomy and dignity: A discussion on contingency and dominance. *Health Care Analysis* 22 (2):174–191.

Van Gennep, A. (1909). *Les rites de passage: Étude systématique des rites*. Paris: Nourry.

Van Leeuwen, P., Geue, D., Thiel, M., Cysarz, C., Lange, S. Romano, M. C., et al. (2009). Influence of paced maternal breathing on fetal–maternal heart rate coordination. *Proceedings of the National Academy of Science USA* 106 (33):13661–13666.

Wittkowski, J. (2004). Sterben und Trauern: Jenseits der Phasen. *Pflege Zeitschrift* 57 (12):2–10.

Wong, P. T. P. (2008). Meaning management theory and death acceptance. In A. Tomer, G. Eliason and P. T. P. Wong (Eds.), *Existential and spiritual issues in death attitudes* (65–87). New York: Erlbaum.

Wright, K., and Flemons, D. (2002). Dying to know: Qualitative research with terminally ill persons and their families. *Death Studies* 26 (3):255–271.

Zimmermann-Acklin, M. (2009). Politischer Umgang mit gegensätzlichen ethischen Positionen am Beispiel der Sterbehilfe. In Gesellschaft für ethische Fragen (Ed.), *Arbeitsblatt*, no. 48 (23–28). Zurich: Gesellschaft für ethische Fragen.

INDEX

Numbers in italics refer to pages on which figures appear.

metaphors / symbols (*continued*)
Well, 55, 140n.4; Hansel and
Gretel, 56; Mother Hulda, 36, 55,
73, 90–92, 139n.1
music therapy, 5, 9, 11, 63–64, 87
musical sensitivity of the dying. *See*
hearing sensitivity
music-assisted relaxation and
imagination, 5, 11, 58, 68, 137n.2;
case narratives, 8–9, 86, 134–135

Nahm, M., 19
nakedness / nothingness (metaphor
and feeling), 37–38, 49, 56–57, 75,
78, 81; case narrative, 38–39
near-death experiences: light in, 27,
46, 58, 87, 105–106; and meaning,
20; and mystery of death, 24–25,
45–46, 126; as similar to spiritual
experiences of the dying, 27, 36,
85, 87, 115; and struggle, 59, 87; and
transformation of perception, 3,
5, 46, 58–59. *See also* ego-distant
perception; consciousness:
endless / nondualistic
near-death sphere. *See*
transition / dying process
needs of the dying: changing,
in transition process, 7, 9–10,
66–69, 109–112; and needs-
based end-of-life care, 2–8,
10, 66, 84, 109–110, 112–114.
See also indication-oriented
approach to end-of-life care;
transition / dying process

Neumann, E., 138n.3
Nissim, R., 2
nothingness, feeling of. *See*
nakedness / nothingness
Nouwen, H., 94
numinous, experience of the:
case narrative, 49–52; eye as
symbol of, 76, 78–79, 81; and
fear, 47–53; and numinous
Other, 51–53, 60, 76, 78–79, 81; as
sound / vibration / atmosphere,
48, 54, 56–57, 64; in transition and
transformation of perception,
59–61

Olson, K. L., 16
Otto, R., 54

pain: and acceptance, 93–95; case
narratives, 8–10; 86, 92–93, 109–111,
134–135; "Dying Is a Transition,"
findings on in, 84, 96, 131, *133*; and
family members and the dying,
114–116; and family problems, 98;
and good dying, 2; music, effects
of, on fear and, 63–64, 86, 134–135;
in post-transition / spiritual
opening, beyond suffering
and, 44–45, 85, 105, 107, 115; in
pre-transition, 26; and primordial
fear, 58, 89; and sedation, 2, 35, 98,
112, 137n.1; in struggle and fear, 89;
and transformation of perception,
65–67, 93–95, 105, 107. *See also*
sedation